WITHDRAWN

# ANCIENT FIELDS

# ANCIENT FIELDS

*A tentative analysis of vanishing
earthworks and landscapes*

BY

H. C. BOWEN

FOR THE RESEARCH COMMITTEE
ON ANCIENT FIELDS

Republished by S R Publishers Ltd 1970

FIRST PUBLISHED BY THE BRITISH ASSOCIATION FOR
THE ADVANCEMENT OF SCIENCE
LONDON S.W.1
1961

Reprinted 1970 by S.R. Publishers Limited,
East Ardsley, Wakefield, Yorkshire, England

ISBN 0 85409 606 X

Reproduced and Printed by Redwood Press Limited,
Trowbridge and London

*Frontispiece*

"Celtic" fields, *Shillingstone Hill, Dorset*; one inch O.S. Sheet 178, Nat. Grid. Ref. 840095. Both low-level oblique air photographs by J. K. St. Joseph. *Crown Copyright reserved.*

(a) From the east. "Celtic" fields in old pasture. "Y" was an enclosure probably contemporary with the fields.

(b) A slightly different view, also from the east, after modern deep ploughing. "X" marks the same spot in both photographs. The track clearly visible as a double line above "X" leads to a contemporary settlement off the picture to the left. It had been re-used and deeply hollowed for part of its length but in places the normal unworn *double-lynchet way* can still be seen.

Comparison of these photographs with those on Plate (I), of the same area, is intended to build up a "portrait" of a site, demonstrate the complementary virtues of different sorts of photograph and help in the interpretation of each.

(a)

(b)

# ANCIENT FIELDS

*A tentative analysis of vanishing
earthworks and landscapes*

BY

H. C. BOWEN

FOR THE RESEARCH COMMITTEE
ON ANCIENT FIELDS

PUBLISHED BY THE BRITISH ASSOCIATION FOR THE
ADVANCEMENT OF SCIENCE
3, Sanctuary Buildings, Gt. Smith St., London, S.W.1

# CONTENTS

NOTE: For the form of reference given in foot-notes to works listed in the bibliography see the note introducing the bibliography.

*First printed 1961*
*Reprinted 1962*
*Reprinted 1963*

# PREFACE

ANCIENT fields still cover very large areas. Most of them are faced with obliteration in the near future, and will no longer be available for study. This booklet has been written in the belief that these remains are important and that we do not know nearly as much as we could about them. Its purpose is to provide an initial analysis of their nature as a starting point for the work that ought to be done on them before it is too late.

It is hoped that serious controversy has been avoided; but account has been taken of considerable unpublished material, particularly from Wessex, and some tentative conclusions have been incorporated because it is highly desirable that they should be tested wherever possible. On the other hand positively no attempt has been made to provide a review of all known sites.

The booklet has been written for the British Association for the Advancement of Science Research Committee on Ancient Fields. This Committee was set up in 1958 as a consequence of the Association's meeting in Dublin in the previous September, when Section H discussed ancient agriculture in north-western Europe (*Advancement of Science*, **56**, March 1958, pp. 365–71). The purpose of the Committee is to promote the study of ancient fields and this booklet is its basic product. The Committee at present consists of: Professor W. F. Grimes, Director of the Institute of Archaeology, University of London (Chairman); Professor C. F. C. Hawkes, Oxford University (founder Chairman); A. Aberg, Southampton Museum; C. W. Phillips, Archaeology Officer, Ordnance Survey; Professor S. Piggott, Edinburgh University; Dr. G. Whittington, University of St. Andrews; Dr. P. D. Wood, Reading University; H. C. Bowen, staff of the Royal Commission on Historical Monuments (England), (Hon. Secretary).

# ACKNOWLEDGMENTS

MY greatest thanks are due to members of the Committee who have borne patiently with requests to comment on drafts and have always been most helpful; to the Royal Commission on Historical Monuments for England—and colleagues past and present on its staff—to whom I owe a great general debt and am particularly grateful for permission to make use of specific information in its files (noted in the text), to base Appendices B and C on tally cards used by its staff, and to reproduce, or use in adapted form, the following illustrations: Figs. 2E, 3 and 4A, and Plates IB and IIB; and to Eric Moss, who most willingly gave his services to draw Figs. 1, 4 and 5 and all but the excavated lynchet section of Fig. 2 at considerable personal inconvenience. I am also particularly grateful to the two scholars who first defined "Celtic" fields and have done more than anyone else to advance our knowledge of them: Dr. O. G. S. Crawford, who gave his support to this project but, sadly, did not live to criticise it; and Dr. E. Cecil Curwen who has been good enough to read the text at a very busy time and has given much-valued advice and encouragement. Others who have most kindly read the text and given valuable opinions and advice include Mr. J. W. Anstee, Mr. G. P. Burstow, Lady Aileen Fox, Dr. W. G. Hoskins, Mr. J. G. Hurst, Mr. A. Jewell, Dr. P. Jewell, Mr. C. A. Ralegh Radford, and Mr. C. Thomas. For all opinions now expressed in the text, however, no-one can be held responsible but the writer.

For advice on particular points my debts are too numerous to recount but I cannot omit that given at many times by Mr. W. T. Hill, Air Photographs Officer of the Ministry of Housing and Local Government, and say also how much I have appreciated the ever-willing help of his staff. I should also like to express gratitude to Mr. F. G. Payne of the Welsh Folk Museum, St. Fagan's, for reading and commenting on the section dealing with ploughs.

For permission to use illustrations not already mentioned I have to thank the Cambridge University Committee in Aerial Photography and the Air Ministry for the frontispiece and Plates I, IV and V, all photographs taken by Dr. J. K. S. St. Joseph, and the Air Ministry also for Plates IA, IIA and III, routine photographs taken by the R.A.F. but of great archaeological value.

# LIST OF PLATES

# LIST OF LINE FIGURES

# CHAPTER I

## *The Importance of Ancient Fields*

AGRICULTURE has been a fundamental activity of man since he left the savage stage and became a barbarian. From that day to this his fields have changed the face of nature. For that reason the study of ancient fields must also take count of quite recent activity and is inextricably bound up with any proper interpretation of large parts of our landscape. In varying degrees it is the concern of all whose interests or research lead to the countryside.

There are, for instance, many ways of studying agrarian history and each contributes to an overall picture. But while the available objects, and (for the later periods) documents which provide the basis for much of this research are safely preserved, perhaps our most important sources of knowledge, the actual remains of the ancient fields and the features associated with them, are being rapidly destroyed. The bulk of them will not be available for investigation much longer. It is the extent of our archaeological heritage which makes this inevitable. Britain is the only country in north-western Europe, apart from Denmark, where there are known to be widespread remains of fields belonging to the prehistoric and Roman periods. Taking the country as a whole, these alone, without considering the also notable spread of later fields, still cover an immeasureably larger area than any other form of earthwork. Whilst, however, the rate of destruction cannot be denied there may be some who will, very rightly, enquire what is the use of studying field remains or, perhaps, challenge the inadequacy of our present knowledge.

To the first of these there are a number of answers but the most important is that the fields are capable of providing information which can be gathered from no other sources. They give a picture of bygone countrysides with their farms—to the location of which the fields sometimes give the best clue—roads and, perhaps just as important, areas which were never tilled. They reflect in different

I

degrees technical equipment, farming method, population and land hunger. They occur frequently in complexes of several periods which provide an opportunity for studying the sequence of types. They are not "just fields" dependent only for their layout on the judgment of individual farmers; they represent conservative and traditional answers to problems of environment, social and economic organisation, and equipment available in different phases. Again, because so widespread, they are involved in relationship with almost every other type of earthwork. Thus, a very great deal of archaeological fieldwork, to be adequate, demands an attempt to understand them.

The inadequacy of our knowledge is best seen when considering what we mean by the three main types of agricultural remains regarded for our purpose here as ancient, that is, "*Celtic*" *fields, strip lynchets* and *ridge-and-furrow*. The very term "Celtic field" is still used only because it is so indefinite, covering as it does all those fields of regular shape which were laid out before the Saxons established themselves in this country.[1] The existence of plough-furrows under burial mounds of the Early Bronze Age on the Continent[2] and the very recent discovery of plough-furrows on actual fields apparently of this period in Cornwall (see p. 9) suggests the possibility of an origin as early as the sixteenth century B.C., while it seems highly likely that some remained in use after the withdrawal of Roman rule in the early fifth century A.D. They take a number of different forms (compare, e.g., the examples on Fig. 3) but all have two things in common: small size and, unless there is some reason for variation, an approximate rectangularity which can proclaim their presence even through the imposed pattern of cultivation according to a different system. As generally found they vary from about $\frac{1}{4}$ acre to $1\frac{1}{2}$ acres in size and in shape range from the approximately square to a rectangle about six times as long as broad. The nature of the field sides and the arrangement of groups, also diverse, is considered in Chapter III. It has not yet been possible to assign narrow periods to any of these forms but some suggestions about development in the

---

[1] Its use does not necessarily imply any connection with the *Celtic system* of agriculture discussed, for instance, by H. L. Gray, *English Field Systems*, pp. 157-271.

[2] A concise account of such finds up to 1950 is given in IV Glob 1951, pp. 123-4.

Roman period are put forward later (p. 24). Other problems will become apparent in the course of ensuing descriptions and some are specified in Appendix A.

*Strip lynchets* are the long narrow, often prominent terraces which, where recorded, have a respectable place on Ordnance Survey maps befitting a form of earthwork that has sculptured so many hillsides from Cornwall to South Scotland. Yet their origins and nature are still the subject of argument. Some were under regular cultivation in the nineteenth century but when they began is much less clear. The arguments for the post-Roman period, which the writer personally accepts, will be put forward later but there are complications in that some were certainly laid out after others, that there was an ebb and flow of cultivation and that regional and local variations undoubtedly exist. In recent years, though there are probably not many people who still believe them to be raised sea-beaches[3] their arable nature has been disputed[4] and alleged examples have been called prehistoric or Roman.[5] Many farmers find it difficult to believe they were fields at all, while popular tradition occasionally allots them special crops. They also differ considerably in arrangement and detail (the height of their scarps, for instance, may vary from inches to 20 ft. or more) but a close definition is necessary (and has been attempted in Chapter IV) if they are not to be taken as merely synonymous with "strip fields", a source of considerable confusion in the past. It is surely possible to arrive at near certainty as to their material origins and use and to refine our views on their development in time, but there must be copious and undeniable evidence to satisfy all and, in any case, to bear witness to the regional or local variations.

*Ridge-and-furrow* is argued about as much as *strip lynchets*, though without any serious doubts about its mode of origin (p. 10). Its chronology and significance are the main problems. It cannot have come into existence until there was a plough capable of building it up. This had occurred at least in a few places well before the Romans

[3] Such a theory is refuted in II Poulett Scrope 1869.
[4] V Orwin 1954, pp. 175–9.
[5] E.g. III Barger 1938, p. 391.

left the country and consequently a view very recently advanced that ridge-and-furrow undeniably existed then cannot be contradicted on those grounds.[6] That ridge-and-furrow surrounds many deserted mediaeval villages is well known, but against the implications of this a wealth of documentation has recently been put forward in support of a largely nineteenth-century origin for the surviving remains.[7] Evidence is rapidly accumulating to show that it covered thousands of acres of high downland far from mediaeval settlement where its existence has not been generally recognised. Once more it is worth while attempting an analysis of these remains to avoid lumping together what is more properly put into separate categories (Chapter IV).

Finally, since *"Celtic" fields, strip lynchets, ridge-and-furrow* and other earthworks are often met together in determinable relationships it is only by investigating these whenever possible that the various relationships will be worked out in a sufficient number of examples to warrant the safe generalisations which are so badly needed.

The most urgent basic aim of present research, bearing in mind the rapid and inevitable rate of destruction, should surely be the production of as many good annotated plans as possible. Methods of tackling this are suggested in Chapter V. Meanwhile, one final point must be made to answer the possible objection that, since we have innumerable air photographs, the record is already preserved for posterity. Experience has amply shown that this is far from enough. We must regard air photography as an absolutely essential tool without which the task could not be attempted at all, but it remains a tool and our knowledge will not be based on secure foundations unless the ground is worked over—by many people, and soon.

[6] III Applebaum, 1958, p. 72.
[7] VI Kerridge, 1951.

# CHAPTER II

## Basic farming practice and Implements

THE implements used in cultivation represent only one of a number of factors which bear on field shape, size and earthwork remains. Nevertheless, there can be no intelligent study of ancient fields unless it is backed by some knowledge of the basic practices of farming and the characteristics of the tools available to carry them out in different periods and places.

Here there is room only to mention some of the points to be borne in mind. Sections (IV–VI) of the bibliography are intended as an introduction to more detailed study.

The basic requirements of agriculture are the same for all periods:

(a) The ground must be broken up,
(b) A seed-bed prepared,
(c) Animals kept away from the growing crops,
(d) The harvest taken,
(e) Crops prepared for storage or use,
(f) Crops stored.

Also, in settled agriculture, manuring and periodic fallowing are essential if adequate crop yields are to be maintained.

(a) and (b) are the most onerous and will tend to determine the size of individual fields, e.g. at what could be ploughed in one day.[1] (c) might be met either by tethering[2]—as in the Channel Islands today —by the construction of enclosed areas or by the constant use of neat-herds and the like. (See also below, on *fallow ground*.) (d) will not be reflected directly in ground remains but it should be remembered that the introduction of the scythe in the Romano-British period *inter alia* facilitated the taking of hay harvests which in turn would make it possible to maintain more stock through the winter. (e) might involve rick-yards amongst the fields as well as in the

[1] E.g. I Pliny, Book XVIII, III, p. 195.
[2] Cf. Joan Thirsk, *Tudor enclosures* (Historical Association pamphlet), p. 17.

5

settlements, also threshing floors, working areas and corn-drying ovens. (*f*) sometimes meant the construction of storage pits for consumption corn, but seed corn always had to be stored in granaries above ground.

*Manure* which came from middens or dumps near settlements often contained datable rubbish which was then scattered over the fields and explains the prehistoric, Roman and occasionally later potsherds that are frequently found, usually much worn and thinly spread, over large areas. (Concentrations of pottery, especially when not abraded, require a different explanation.)

*Marling* and the *spreading of chalk* were other means of keeping the land in good heart. (See p. 31 below.)

*Fallow ground*: the necessity to rest the land meant that only a proportion (anciently perhaps one-half or one-third) was likely to be under crop at one time. A settlement would always require much more land than was needed to maintain it in any one year. The implications of this are further considered on p. 33 (pasture).

To return to (*a*) and (*b*), *breaking-up the ground* and *preparing a seed-bed*, it is clear that the implements used may be related to the likely size and proportions of the fields and will certainly have affected the nature and rate of earth movement within each field. All disturbance of the soil on slopes will tend to produce lynchets, that is, scarps, on the edges of such disturbance but different implements are likely to cause little or much movement and some can even be used to retard it by the turning of a slice against the slope, if not too steep.

The implements include *digging-sticks*, *hoes*, *spades and caschroms* and *ploughs*. Digging-sticks may be no more than pointed sticks thrust through holes in circular stone-weights, tending to produce, or at least not be inconvenient for use in, plots with curving edges. Others may be much more effective and, like some paddle-shaped examples recorded amongst modern primitive tribes in the East Indies, be capable of producing furrows as straight and strong as those of a plough.[3] Of such wooden implements there are no known early remains. It seems probable that antler tines, which were certainly

[3] *A.*, **XXXI** (March 1957), pp. 39–40.

employed as digging tools, may have been used as hoes even from the Neolithic period and there are illustrations of metal hoes in Egypt from the early second millennium B.C.,[4] but the earliest recognisable hoes (of iron) in this country appear to be of Roman date. There is little doubt that some fields (as apart from garden plots) were at that time still being tilled with an implement of this sort if the slope was much over 20 degrees (see Plate III, for example).

*Caschroms* and *spades* and the like come into the category of implements which turn a slice and it might be said of the caschrom, at least, that it is more closely related to the heavy plough than would allow it to be considered as ancestral to the light plough! It is indeed a foot-plough which always turns the earth in one direction, accelerating lynchet formation. (An excellent drawing showing its action appears in III Curwen 1946.) *Spades* are also sometimes used to invert slices and produce ridges, though quite different in nature from *ridge-and-furrow* (see Fig. 5B and p. 47 *lazy beds*).

*Ploughs* fall into two main classes: *light ploughs* or *ards*, and *heavy ploughs*.[5]

*Light ploughs* have only one part operating on the soil—a share of wood, perhaps iron-tipped, or of iron. They have been classified in different ways. A *sole* ard ("crook" ard) has a plough-beam and horizontal sole in one piece and is the simplest form. A *beam* ard ("bow" or "spade" ard) has stilt and share, or shares, inserted through a hole near the base of the plough-beam (see Fig. 1). Both types were highly manoeuvrable and could be lifted off the ground with ease by one man. Human traction might have been used in awkward sites. Despite this a two-ox team seems to have been normal. The *beam ard*, at least, seems to have been capable of cutting quite wide and deep furrows and with its arrow-shaped share tilted could move soil to one side but could not turn a sod effectively in the same way as a heavy plough. It could not therefore build significant ridges. Whether *cross-ploughing* was necessary or not the evidence of

[4] IV Singer 1954, Vol. I, pp. 539 ff.

[5] The distinction is in one sense an arbitrary one because there can be both light and heavy "heavy" ploughs—but the study of these implements is a specialised one and the reader is earnestly referred to the bibliography.

# FIG. 1. THE PLOUGH AND ITS ACTION

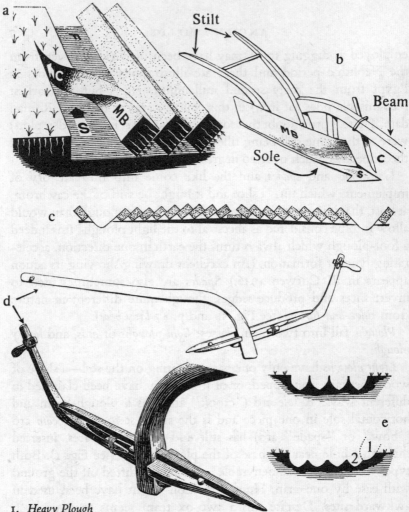

1. *Heavy Plough*

   a. The slice is cut vertically by the coulter (C), undercut by the share (S) and turned by the mould-board (M.B.) (Based on H. Stephens: *Book of the Farm, 1871*.) (F) is the furrow.

   b. Diagram shewing parts of a plough.

   c. A plough-ridge in course of formation, second gathering before harrowing. (A *turn-wrest* plough would lay the slices *one-way* only.)

2. *Light Plough*

   d. "Beam" type, based on a replica of the Donneruplund *ard* made in the Museum of English Rural Life, Reading. Note complexity, e.g. how fore-share fits on top of arrow-shaped main share.

   e. Upper diagram shows effect of side-by-side furrows with *ard* upright. Lower shows the unploughed slivers broken down by ploughing with the ard alternately tilted (1) and then remaining upright (2) in the same furrow. Based on IV Steensberg 1957/8 with the kind approval of Professor Steensberg.

*prehistoric plough furrows* suggests that ploughing in different directions was practised. Very recently (1960) such furrows have been exposed by excavation of a group of Bronze Age fields probably datable to the sixteenth century B.C. and onwards, at Gwithian, Cornwall. Considerable ploughing of the sandy soil was indicated by foot-high lynchets but the plough pattern was in places curiously uncomplicated. The furrows, which had bitten up to 3 inches into the sub-soil, were triangular in section and often in close-set pairs each of which was 18 inches or more apart. These were crossed at right angles by similar furrows. It seems clear that such remains do not represent the total plough-movement required to cultivate these fields even once, yet the marks are not the result of chance "biting" by the plough. They seem indeed to indicate a pattern of deliberate wide-spaced deep furrowing.[6] By contrast it has recently been demonstrated by Dr. Steensberg that in ordinary ploughing the same furrows might have been ploughed twice, as described by Columella, once with the ard upright and once, to deepen the furrow and to break down the soil between furrows and throw the soil to one side, with it sloping (see Fig. 1E).[7] Either cross-ploughing or this technique would double the work and thus tend to keep the fields small.

Evidence for the use of light ploughs in this country comes almost entirely from the finding of iron shares, none in pre-Iron Age association, but wooden parts (of two beam ards) have been found in Scotland.[8] Otherwise our knowledge is largely derived from complete ards found in Danish bogs.

A *type of plough that might be regarded as intermediate* between the light and the heavy plough emerges in the Roman period. The share is fitted with "ears" and "ground-wrests" on either side. While the

[6] I am much indebted to Mr. Charles Thomas for permission to include this description which does scant justice to the series he has uncovered, so far unique in Britain. He hopes to publish a short illustrated account in the Proceedings of the West Cornwall Field Club this year (1961).

[7] IV Steensberg 1957-8, pp. 157-62. For an account of a recent ploughing experiment with a reconstructed Donneruplund *ard* see *A.*, XXXIV 1960, pp. 144-7.

[8] Milton Loch, Kircudbrightshire, *P.S.A.S.*, LXVII (1952-3), pp. 143-4 and Lochmaben, Dumfriesshire. *A.H.R.*, V (1957), p. 74.

function of the "ears" was probably to clear the furrow it seems likely that they could, if the plough was tilted, throw the soil to either side as required.

The *heavy ploughs* we are concerned with have at least two parts which operate on the soil: a *coulter* shaped like a knife to cut the sod vertically and, just behind it, a *share*, which usually has a "wing" on one side to under-cut effectively. A *mould-board* of wood which turns the sod right over has also been present since the Roman period (Fig. 1). There has probably always been a considerable variety of types to deal with local conditions and requirements. Wheels are not essential[9] but before recent centuries all heavy ploughs probably had rectangular frames. A fixed-mould-board plough always turns the sod to the same side in relation to itself and coulters usually had blades asymmetrically "set" to facilitate this. Such a plough can only be used in one of two ways: to plough (*a*) *in parallel ridges*, (*b*) *round-and-round*.

The process of *ridge ploughing* is shown in Figs. 1 and 5. The "headland", i.e. the turning area at each end of the ridges, is ploughed last of all. A series of parallel ridges is usually employed rather than one vast ridge (whereby each half of the field would be ploughed so that the sods lay towards the central spine) to save the great waste that would be involved by the plough having to move "free" (i.e. without ploughing) along the ever-increasing gap between the furrow ends.

The technique of ridge ploughing does not necessarily entail the building up of enduring earthen ridges—simply because a single "gathering-up" is insufficient and the next ploughing is often intended to break the process, e.g. by ploughing furrows down the incipient ridges (as is done in the surviving strip fields at Laxton, Notts.) or just by cross-ploughing. The inference follows, therefore, that when ridges are found they have either been built up intentionally or have been accepted as the result of ploughing with a

---

[9] But after describing coulter and shares, Pliny states that the fitting of small wheels to a plough was an invention made "not long ago" (i.e. not later than the first half of the first century A.D.) in *Raetia Galliae*, I Pliny Book XVIII, p. 297. Cf. IV Aberg 1956–7, p. 181.

fixed-mould-board plough within a rigid pattern of strips where it was not practicable to alter the position of the furrows.

The *round-and-round* technique, despite its name, is normally associated with fields whose sides are perfectly straight. It is begun by ploughing an isolated ridge in the middle of the field on the line of its long axis. The plough then continues to build a four-sided figure outwards from this centre, turning each time along a line which is a diagonal from the original ridge-end to a corner of the field (see Fig. 5). The method may well have been used occasionally in "Celtic" fields. In modern times it produces a strong mark on the line of the diagonals which is sometimes accentuated by the refinement of then ploughing along these lines as a tidying-up operation.[10] This method is frequently used when downland is newly broken up and is responsible for the most pronounced of the "envelope" patterns so often seen on air photographs. (Others are caused by the processes of cropping.)

The first good evidence for the existence of *heavy ploughs* in this country is in the Romano-British period and derives from the finding of coulters and winged shares mostly (but not exclusively) in "villas" and towns. The fact that some of the coulters have a clear "set" shows that they were intended to turn a slice to one side and it is virtually certain that mould-boards were also used.[11] Despite this innovation there is little doubt that light ploughs remained in common use.

*One-way ploughs* ("turnwrest" ploughs) have movable mouldboards and coulters enabling the sod always to be turned in the same direction in relation to the field whichever way the plough was pointing.[12] They are expressly designed to avoid the building of ridges and thus their use in the reploughing of fields belonging to an earlier system is less easy to detect than if ridges were left. It will in fact most often be suggested by the creation of new lynchet lines

[10] It is possible to call the method "square ploughing" but in this context the term might be even more misleading. Cf. W. Fream, *Elements of Agriculture*, 13th Ed., revised by D. H. Robinson, pp. 108–9.

[11] IV Payne 1957, p. 78.

[12] IV Nightingale 1953.

just above old *positive* lynchets or below old *negative* lynchets (Fig. 5D and p. 21 below).

*Plough teams.* The capacity of draught animals to pull a long furrow was assessed very pessimistically by Columella: "to run a furrow more than 120 feet is very injurious to a beast." It is a fact that many "Celtic" field sides are no longer but this is scarcely the reason, since 120 feet would only be about eight times the length of the equipment, and reads strangely against his further advice that the ploughman "should not stop in the middle of a furrow but should allow a rest at the end of it, so that the ox will exert himself more energetically the whole way in the hope of stopping"![13] Walter of Henley might be allowed to comment from the thirteenth century: "the horse or ox must be very poor that cannot from the morning go easily in pace 3 leagues from his starting place and return by 3 o'clock."[14]

The two-ox team is commonly shown in rock drawings of the Late Bronze Age on the Continent. Others are also shown and there were certainly variations, including, no doubt, human traction, but the short straight sides of most "Celtic" fields strongly support the idea of a team that was at any rate small and mobile.

In the mediaeval period, although the universal use of an eight-ox team is no longer accepted—some being smaller and some, though rarely, even larger[15]—an equipage much more cumbersome than that usual for the light ploughs of prehistoric and Romano-British times was undoubtedly normal. Economic use therefore required longer furrows since turning was a more cumbersome business, and whatever the type of heavy plough it would by its nature also involve either a lot of unproductive movement on the headlands or a halt, in the case of a turn-wrest, for the readjustment of the "shifting-ear" and coulter. It may be added that the sinuous, usually reversed-"S", curve sometimes seen in mediaeval field patterns has been credibly interpreted as directly due to the use of a long team.[16]

[13] I Columella I, p. 127.        [14] VI Lamond 1890, p. 9.
[15] H. G. Richardson, *History*, XXVI (Mar. 1942), pp. 287–94; R. Lennard, *E.H.R.*, LX (1945), pp. 217–33, and LXXV (April 1960), pp. 193–207.
[16] VI Eyre 1955.

Knowledge of the *type of corn* grown in the prehistoric period is derived from carbonised grain (probably charred by accident when parching) and from the impress of grain in pottery. Dr. Helbaek has suggested that *spelt*, a particular form of wheat, was introduced in the Iron Age and that it was a winter-sown crop.[17]

As a very rough guide the actual *corn yield* in the Iron Age and Romano-British periods is reasonably assessed at about 10 bushels per acre. This is about a third of the modern yield on chalk. Perhaps 3 of the 10 bushels would be put on one side for seed. The annual consumption per head in modern times is $4\frac{1}{2}$ bushels. When it is remembered that the requirements of a Roman legion would have been around 500 bushels a week[18] we have one good reason for the undoubted increase of "Celtic" fields in the Roman period.

[17] IV Helbaek 1952, p. 208.
[18] S. Piggott in *Roman and Native in North Britain* (1958). Ed. I. A. Richmond, Chap. I.

# CHAPTER III

# *"Celtic" Field Remains*

## DISTRIBUTION

THE Third Edition of the O.S. map of Roman Britain indicates the surviving distribution of whatever date. Many groups appear on ordinary O.S. maps. (See also Sections VII to XV of the Bibliography and for a discussion of the possible relationship of these recoverable bounds to the former limits of cultivation see III Clark 1952, pp. 98–9.)

## ORIGINAL MARKING-OUT

So far as is known "Celtic" fields represent the first imposition of a regular cultivation pattern on the landscape in this country. Despite piecemeal development most were undoubtedly at first marked out on the ground. The method just as undoubtedly varied and often, it seems, was so temporary as to leave no trace of its nature; but examples of recognisable form include:

   i. Small banks with ditches (the latter, 2 feet wide and 1 foot deep have been found under spread banks in Denmark.[1])

   ii. Low banks—not infrequently found either running against the contour or on flat ground. Some might have been scraped-up, others be no more than baulks marked out in some temporary fashion and sharpened on either side by ploughing.

   iii. Lines of stones e.g. Skomer Island, Pembrokeshire, or, as on Dartmoor, upright slabs carefully set up.[2]

[1] XVIII Hatt 1951, pp. 57, 151 and Fig. 35.
[2] XV Grimes 1952, pp. 1–20; IX Fox 1954 and *Trans. Devon. Assoc.*, 86 (1954) p. 26.

iv. Crumbled drystone-rubble walls—usually grass covered (e.g. on Charmy Down, near Bath,[3] and, probably, south of Kingston, Dorset, Plate III.[4] Both on limestone).

Surface stones along the boundary can of course be no more than the result of clearance, though they might have been deliberately used to revet a scarp as it grew. Certainly flints—a hindrance to the plough—were gathered from fields when in cultivation and are often found in such large numbers on the boundaries that countrymen needing rubble frequently dug for them there.[5] Occasionally small mounds of flints are found on or below lynchets, usually at field angles.

The identification of any marking-out feature is important, not least because it might contain dating evidence, but there is a fundamental difference between marker lines and walls, and the latter form a specially interesting subject for investigation. In other areas the probable use of wattle for temporary enclosure of stock and protection of crops must always be borne in mind though it will rarely be proved.

*Lynchets* (Fig. 2). Whatever the original bounds the most characteristic remains on slopes today are "lynchets". This word seems to derive from the Anglo-Saxon "hlinc", "a ridge", but to avoid confusion it is important to restrict its use to arable scarps and to note that *strip lynchets* is a term that must be reserved for a special form of strip *field* bounded by lynchets. (See next chapter.) These scarps are due to the movement of soil caused by the action of cultivation whether it be by hoe or plough of any sort, gravity and the elements playing an important part. One-way ploughing will add to the effect and a heavy plough, especially one that turns a slice constantly downhill, will greatly accelerate the process. The most commonly accepted theory of formation is as follows. Constant tilling of a field will cut a sharp line under its uphill edge(s). This is called the "*negative lynchet*". Downhill the corresponding accumulation on the edge(s) is called the "*positive lynchet*". Most lynchets,

[3] VIII Grimes 1960, p. 223.

[4] VIII R.C.H.M., Vol. II, forthcoming. The O.S. air photograph has also been published in *Luftbild und Vorgeschichte* (a pre-war Luft Hansa publication, the English sites contributed by O. G. S. Crawford) and by R. H. Hodgkin, *History of the Anglo-Saxons*, Vol. I, opposite p. 39.       [5] II Cunnington 1869.

# FIG. 2. LYNCHET FORMATION

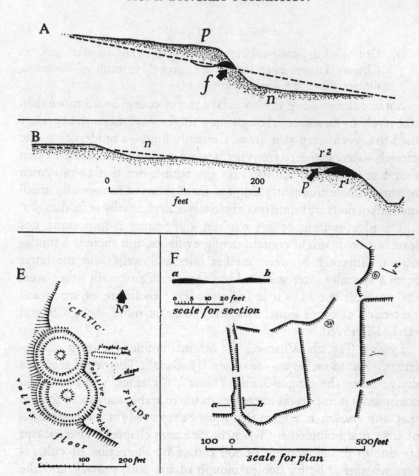

A. *Theory.* Positive lynchet (*p*) is distinct from, and above, negative (*n*). A marking out bank (*f*) ensures this (not to scale).

B. *Complication* (after E. C. Curwen). A hillfort bank ($r^1$) (Cissbury) retains the positive lynchet which is masked by a new rampart ($r^2$) when the hillfort is re-used as such.

C. *Variation with Interpretation* (Wylye Down, Wilts.)
   (i to iii not to scale)

   i. The field edge is marked out by a very slight scraping up, mostly turf and top soil.

   ii. After some seasons plough soil piles over this slight feature and dribbles downhill, covering the negative lynchet which has already cut a scarp in the subsoil (chalk).

   iii. The process continues, the lower field edge drawing away from the upper as the negative lynchet deepens and is covered by spill from above, as well as stones gathered from the fields. (N.B. in the diagram the various features are exaggerated deliberately to make this interpretation clear).

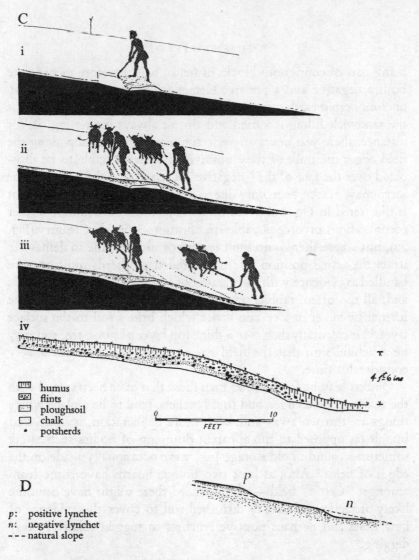

C

i

ii

iii

iv

humus
flints
ploughsoil
chalk
• potsherds

4 f⁻ 6 ins

$0$                    $10$
FEET

D

P

n

p:  positive lynchet
n:  negative lynchet
- - - natural slope

iv.  The final lynchet section shows spill from above (i.e. positive lynchet) almost as deep over the face of the scarp as above it.

D.  *Double lynchet track (not to scale).* Laid out with the fields. If it had been inserted below a pre-existing lynchet there would be a negative element in the uphill scarp.

E.  *Curving lynchet lines.* Formed by the piling of ploughsoil against earthworks already existing (disc barrows, Grafton, Wilts.—based on a R.C.H.M. plan). Cf. Plate II(a).

F.  *Curving lynchet lines* without certain explanation but not determined by the topography. Due to the existence of settlement palisades ? Figures ringed give scarp heights in feet.

being part of contiguous blocks of fields, will therefore incorporate both a negative and a positive element. The concept is one of an uncomplicated earthy sandwich, but it tends to obscure the fact that the sandwich filling is varied and almost always interesting. If, for instance, there was never any effective barrier to soil-slip along the field edges the bulk of the "positive" lynchet is liable to be dissipated over the face of the "negative" scarp so that the height of the scarp may, in fact, be mainly due to this negative element. The point is illustrated in Fig. 2C, based on a very recent excavation.[6] Other complications involve possible stratification, as inside Cissbury (Fig. 2B), but where there is no built feature or old turf line to demarcate strata the actual position of small abraded potsherds must only be handled as evidence with the greatest of suspicious care. Earthworms and, all too often, rabbits tend to stir the contents of lynchets, the former however in a certain order which brings soil to the surface layer.[6a] Incidentally therefore a thick top layer of stone-free soil may be a helpful sign that the field has not been ploughed for a very considerable time.

Objects may be found other than those that have been spread with the manure. Field edges, and thus lynchets, tend to be a place where things are thrown away and, with more deliberation, it seems that burials (as opposed to the apparent dumping of bodies such as are sometimes found in old storage pits) were occasionally made on the edges of fields.[7] Also, at least two bronze hoards have come from amongst "Celtic" fields—where indeed there might have been the likely attraction of already disturbed soil to cover the evidence of new holes and perhaps positive lynchets to suggest relatively easy digging.[8]

---

[6] Undertaken by Mr. J. W. G. Musty and the writer with members of the Salisbury Museum Excavation Sub-Committee.

[6a] See, for instance, P. Jewell in the "*Times*" *Science Review*, Winter 1959, p. 18; also his "Natural History and Experiment in Archaeology", *A. of S.*, 59 (Dec. 1958), pp. 165–72.

[7] E.g. inurned, near Lewes, Sussex. Sx. A.C., LXXV, pp. 254–7.

[8] Lulworth, Dorset. Exact location uncertain. *Ant. J.*, XV, p. 449. Ebbesbourne Wake, Wiltshire, buried in the surface of a field, not a lynchet. *W.A.M.*, LIII, pp. 104–12. Cf. p. 37 footnote 32.

The rate of lynchet formation clearly depends upon the degree of slope, the nature and depth of the soil, the climate (exceptionally heavy rain, though infrequent, can play a big part in a century!), whether any action was taken to counteract it (in historic times soil has often been carted uphill to replace the effects of what is in fact, erosion), any rotation that was practised, and the nature of the implements used. The difficulty of allowing for many of these factors makes it correspondingly difficult to assess the final factor which would be of so much interest—the duration of time under the plough. Observation of modern lynchet formation is of interest but controlled experiment might ultimately teach much more. Lynchet *depth* within one field side occasionally varies and usually increases towards the downhill end. (Fig. 5C.) This must surely be due to accumulation of the positive lynchet, which in such cases, for reasons that it would be interesting to discover, did not spill over the negative.

Very deep lynchets bounding small fields such as in Fig. 3, where the scarps on a north-facing slope were up to 6 feet high, suggest the possibility of deliberate terracing, but this has not yet been established in the "Celtic" phase.

A trackway, perhaps in origin defined by banks, is known as a "*double lynchet track*" when it is bounded by arable scarps. If contemporary with the original layout of the fields it will have a positive lynchet piled against the uphill side and a negative cut away below it (Fig. 2D) but if superimposed it may have a negative element in the uphill scarp. (This must not be confused with the effects of secondary ploughing in some "post-Celtic" period which will usually be distinguishable when the pattern as a whole is considered.) A track which has been deliberately cut out on a steep untilled slope should therefore be termed "terraceway" to make the distinction.

## FRAGMENTARY OR MISLEADING SCARPS

Certain scarps might be caused by the treading and rooting of animals, particularly pigs, which could also produce a mixed soil suggestive of cultivation. Animal refuse, "bedding" and the like might also contribute. Natural features to beware of—but usually only from a distance—include soil slip and, in certain areas, stepped rock formations.

Fragmentary remains may be revealed in the profile of existing banks or walls built over ancient lynchets otherwise lost to cultivation in the new fields thus marked out. Occasionally a sliver of unploughed ground in an arable field will betray the presence of a scarp too massive to make destruction worth while. Before they finally disappear however—and they do ultimately disappear without trace—lynchets are usually seen as long rolling scarps best viewed from uphill to get the advantage of foreshortening, the line of break in slope often detectable by alternately stooping and standing. Unusually long and deep scarps can be due to the tumbling together of the elements of a "double-lynchet track".

Sometimes it is possible to detect the former existence of "Celtic" fields even under well-developed "strip lynchets" and the best clue to this is in short lengths of lynchets differing in height *within* the run of single strip lynchets and clearly therefore due to some earlier formation. Once these are detected confirmatory signs are sometimes forthcoming in slight breaks of slope in the strip lynchets as they cross lines at right angles to the ends of these short lynchets. (See Plate IV.)

### PATTERNS AND RELATIONSHIPS

The following notes are intended to comment, firstly, on the plans of "Celtic" fields individually and in groups and, secondly, on whole farms, including features that might be in association with the fields, both contemporary and otherwise.

Almost all "Celtic" fields have the common characteristics of small size and approximately rectangular shape, though odd examples—e.g. triangular or polygonal—can be found. All have straight sides unless there is some special reason for variation. Yet within these generalisations individual fields do differ considerably in size—from, say $\frac{1}{4}$ to $1\frac{1}{2}$ acres, while their sides may range from *c.* 22 yards to *c.* 160 yards, and the proportions from square to about six to one. (These precise figures are ventured because anything outside them should be given very careful study to be sure that they are not due to interference in some later phase.) In groups their diversity is just as great.

Clearly these matters will always, to some extent, be determined by the ground or such things as situation relative to a settlement, when special usages may be reflected. The primitive undoubtedly survived to neighbour the progressive while the most progressive forms doubtless existed in areas where subsequent settlement has long destroyed all traces. But the three reasons in particular which render typology difficult also reinforce the need to analyse closely.

They are:

i. development and alteration of plan during the "mainstream" of "Celtic" development, probably culminating in the tilling of almost all these fields in the Romano-British period.

ii. ploughing within and over "Celtic" fields in historic periods— much more frequent than is perhaps generally appreciated.

iii. the fact that our best-preserved remains are on slopes where the pattern may not be typical. (See e.g. Plate III, where the fields to the left of the group, though certainly Iron Age or Romano-British, were surely hoe-tilled on an unploughable slope of well over 20 degrees, their long axes straight up and down the slope and altogether different in form from those contemporary fields on the plateau above.)

## POST-ROMAN USE OF DOWNLAND

It seems to the writer that a very high proportion indeed of the downland has been utilised for arable purposes since the days of "Celtic" fields. Some of this appears to be mediaeval, some may be Saxon, but a great deal belongs to later periods. When ridges are left this intrusion is demonstrable—and is discussed in the next chapter. When there is only a broken pattern of fields small clues have to be looked for. These will usually depend upon secondary lynchet lines unconformable with those of the "Celtic" phase. Possibilities are suggested in Fig. 5D. The point is made here because it is vital to all analysis. It clearly bears on the distinction between an enlargement of fields recognised as such and secondary ploughing

within areas of "Celtic" fields where the nature of these old remains
was probably not recognised except as physical obstacles some of
which could be broken down or ploughed-over and some of which
were too massive, or otherwise inconvenient, for destruction.

Despite all the above, clearly distinctive forms of "Celtic" fields
do recur and when many more critical and accurate plans are available the full value of this fact can be analysed. Meanwhile, it seems
that a study of field typology has three main uses: to provide labels
to assist in thinking about the problem, to make the incongruous
stand out, and to see whether there are regional or cultural differences.

## INDIVIDUAL FIELDS

It is sometimes dangerous to classify purely on the basis of shape and
size but the following three forms are put forward as at least being
clearly distinguishable from each other and to have intrinsic
significance.

*Curvilinear plots.* These do not come under the heading of "Celtic"
fields but although, at the moment, their range of date is uncertain
some might be contemporary. They are of irregular form but a
much more detailed study is necessary to see how far groups in
different parts of the country are comparable or to what extent in
any given area they can be broken down into significant classes.
They are well known, for instance, in north-east Yorkshire and on
Dartmoor.[9] Their "lynchets" may be due to the treading of stock
but, if arable, seem much more likely to be connected with the use
of a pointed digging tool than with a plough.

*Small square fields.* Fig. 3B shows fifteen fields in 5 acres planned
by the Royal Commission on Historical Monuments (England)
before their virtual destruction. Some of the former field sides have
been broken down, but they suggest a type—if found in reasonable
numbers—that might be defined by a size of, at most, $\frac{1}{2}$ acre and
approximating to the square. They are undated but in the sense that
fields such as these seem occasionally to have been thrown together
within the "Celtic" phrase there is a suggestion that they were

---

[9] XII Elgee 1930, pp. 129–60. III Curwen 1927, p. 282.

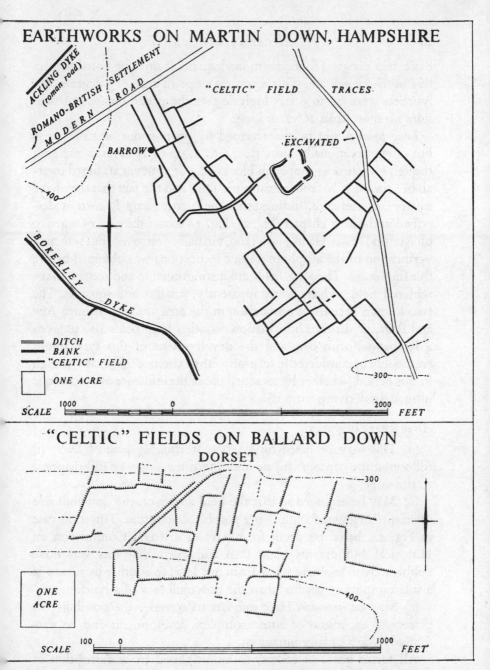

FIG. 3. A. Earthworks on Martin Down, Hants. Plan by R.C.H.M.(Eng.).
*Crown copyright reserved.* See p. 24.

B. "Celtic" fields on Ballard Down, Studland, Dorset. Plan by
R.C.H.M.(Eng.). *Crown copyright reserved.* See p. 24.

basic, that progress found them inadequate. It must be noted that on this north-facing site, with a natural slope of some 15 degrees, the lynchets were up to 6 feet high despite the predominance of field sides no more than 26 yards long.

*Long fields* might be characterised by proportions of 4 or 5 to 1 but only exceptionally more than 6 to 1, up to $1\frac{1}{2}$ acres in size and, though sometimes grouped in blocks of 4 or 5, never arranged overall in "furlongs" of mediaeval type. This, and the fact that they have square enclosed ends, distinguishes them from *strip lynchets* as described in the next chapter (Fig. 4). Fig. 3A shows the plan of a group on Martin Down, Hants., now, too, virtually destroyed, but sufficient verification of the air photographic indications was obtained before this final stage. The long fields are distinguishable and seem to have replaced fields which were, apparently, smaller and squarish. The two known periods of occupation in the area are Late Bronze Age and Romano-British. Information on other long fields also suggests a Romano-British date and the development of this type might reasonably be considered in relation to the existence of a heavy plough in this period (whether by its actual use or the influence of a technique ultimately deriving from it).

## Arrangement in groups

(*a*) This may be based on a series of roughly *parallel lines*: (i) following the contour; (ii) up and down the slope, or (iii) diagonal to the slope.

(*b*) May be arranged so that the field angles on the downhill side overlap. "Staggered angles" is a possible description. This is the case in Fig. 4A, based on detail from part of a Royal Commission on Historical Monuments plan. It is suggested that this was done deliberately to facilitate access from one level to another by means of a side ramp more gradual than the downhill face of a lynchet.

(*c*) May be *irregular*. Here one has to consider the possibility of piecemeal expansion or some complex development and be particularly wary of later intrusions.

All forms need, of course, to be amplified by a description of situation and qualified by field sizes.

# FIG. 4. ACCESS TO FIELDS

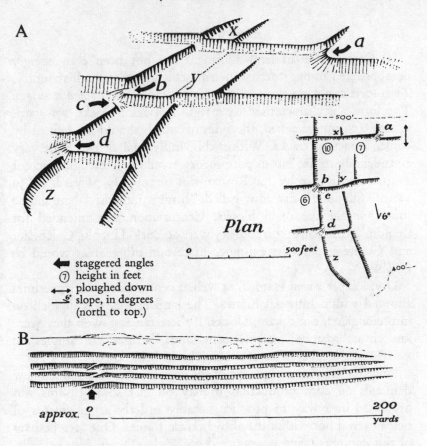

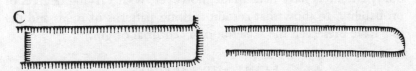

A. Oblique view of "Celtic" field group whose plan is shown to the right.
(a), (b) and (d) are "staggered angles" and (c), also, seems to be a natural way
from one field level to the other. (z), a curved lynchet, is associated with a
small enclosure not shown and is probably part of a settlement.

Figures in circles represent lynchet heights in feet; the single-headed arrow
and figure the slope in degrees and the double-headed arrow a lynchet that
has been broken down.

Based on part of a plan by R.C.H.M.(Eng.).

B. Diagram of contour *strip-lynchets*. Arrow shows ramps joining treads. See p. 41.

C. *Left:* a "Celtic" *long field* with square end. (Cf. p. 24.)
*Right:* The curved end (it may turn either way) sometimes found in *strip-lynchets* which do not "run out".

Not to scale.

(d) Official Roman land allotment has not been convincingly demonstrated amongst actual ancient fields anywhere in this country. Two sorts could exist: *centuriation* and division *per scamna et strigas*. The former is characterised by a rigid layout of blocks, 776 yards square (400 square actus), the sides of which should be defined by banks, stones or tracks. Within this, individual fields might vary considerably in size but in pure theory would be rectangles each of 2 square actus (240 by 120 Roman feet or roughly 78 yards by 39 yards). Subsidiary divisions called "limites intercisivi" might be found within the main blocks. Centuriation was intended for "coloni" (coloniae in this country were at York, Lincoln, Colchester and Gloucester) but its existence in certain other areas would be feasible.[10]

Division *per scamna et strigas* as well as centuriation was sometimes adopted within Imperial Estates. The land in this was divided up into elongated, not square, blocks. If these ran east–west they were known as "scamna" and if north–south "strigae". Examples are known of a local systems of measurement being used.[11]

Since the Roman occupation of the country imposed sudden new demands on corn production it may be that some of this was organised in a way to produce notably orderly arrangements of fields even if not within the above classic frames. One area perhaps of this nature is being investigated on Wylye Down west of Salisbury. Attempts have been made, however, with varying degrees of probability, to show that certain existing patterns of roads and the like have preserved the skeleton of a centurial origin.[12]

## FARMS AND FEATURES

*Settlements*

While the arable fields cover the greatest area it is obvious that their real importance only emerges when they can be related to the settlements that farmed them. These also vary greatly in plan and

---

[10] See especially note by C. E. Stevens in III Nightingale 1952.

[11] Daremberg et Saglio, *Dictionnaire des Antiquités*, I, part 2, 113–14; III, part 2, 963; IV, part 2, 1112–13. XX Bradford 1957, Chap. IV.

[12] E.g. Nightingale, *op. cit.* See also Sx. A.C., LXXXI, pp. 31–41.

here an attempt can only be made to give some clues to identification.

(i) In the highland zone the remains of settlement include stone structures, relatively conspicuous and difficult to level, as on Dartmoor, and much less obvious (and easily obliterated) palisade trenches for timber structures, as recently discovered in Scotland and the north of England.[13] In chalk country, again, although there are many clear and well-preserved earthworks, other settlement remains are often very slight. Their apparent absence, therefore, in a large area of fields can only be regarded as a fact if the fields themselves are well preserved and if the ground has been meticulously searched both on air photographs and on foot.

(ii) The field pattern itself can help. It might break unaccountably, or the fields might become smaller, more irregular, or radiate around a given area. Curved scarp lines are highly suggestive of the former existence of curved palisades which the plough had to respect. These scarps should therefore (if not entirely due to occupational build-up) be either entirely positive or entirely negative lynchets, depending on the lie of the slope. An untested example is shown in Fig. 2F side by side with the plan of a site where curved lynchet lines are explained by surviving earthworks—in this case disc barrows—against which the fields lie.

(iii) Settlements are sometimes found actually *on fields* that had gone out of use. In one such case (Nether Cerne, Dorset, R.C.H.M. Dorset II, forthcoming) advantage had been taken of a pre-existing lynchet to throw up a slight bank from an internal ditch on its edge so that a considerable external scarp was obtained with the minimum of trouble.

(iv) Tracks are useful pointers (see Frontispiece) but not all settlements have recognisable tracks leading to them, e.g. Plate III where only one of the two settlements has its own service track approaching it. Otherwise settlements are quite frequently found adjacent to, or at the junction of, "through" tracks. (See again Fig. 2F.) Occasionally a "switch" track will lead in from a main route.

(v) Ditched or scraped-up earthwork *enclosures*. These are usually obvious, as in the case of the Late Iron Age and Romano-British

[13] XVI R.C.A.M. 1956, p. 19.

settlements in Cranborne Chase, Dorset (so thoroughly excavated by Pitt Rivers),[14] but the diversity of their form and the reason for it is something that deserves a close study.

### Single homesteads inside large enclosures

These are characteristic of *one* type of settlement in the Iron Age.

*Little Woodbury*, near Salisbury, is the type site, though it had been flattened under the strips of a downland open field system long before the brilliant excavation by Dr. Bersu in 1939.[15] Features of Little Woodbury that recur in conjunction on other sites are sub-rectangular or roughly rounded enclosed areas of some 3 to 6 acres bounded by a single ditch, other ditches flaring outwards from near the entrance, pits, working hollows and evidence for one or two large round houses—so comparison should be close before a site is called "a Little Woodbury". There are very few examples so far recognised in association with fields.

(vi) *Complexes* of, e.g., *small platforms* (usually dug into a slope, and built up on the downhill side to act as hut foundations or working areas), sinkings (over storage pits), *hut circles* and *other enclosures* with slight banks and ditches. Settlements such as these may vary from under one to, say, 6 acres in area. (In the chalk and limestone country they present a nucleated aspect but in certain areas, e.g. Dartmoor, the huts are usually more scattered amongst the fields.)

It is sometimes found, as in the case of flint-packed field banks, that quarrying provides a clue to their existence and, indeed, sinkings about the original settlement might have suggested to later people that digging had already taken place and was therefore likely to be profitable.

(vii) *Hillforts*. A distinction must be drawn between hillforts of up to say 6 acres that might be massively defended homesteads akin to Little Woodbury in origin, where a direct relationship with fields could be expected, and larger hillforts whose function was probably more complex. It is interesting to speculate whether the apparent

[14] And reconsidered in VIII Hawkes and Piggott 1947.
[15] VIII Bersu 1940.

absence of "Celtic" fields around some of them might not be due to the desire to preserve open ground for military reasons. "Celtic" fields inside hillforts are likely to be Romano-British in date but are perhaps more interesting if in such a situation they can be proved to be earlier than the hillfort.

## ASSOCIATED FEATURES

Contiguous earthworks are not, of course, always contemporary and certainly on the downland there is little evidence for the levelling of earthwork remains (other than fields) in pre-Roman times. This results in "Celtic" fields often being found around earlier earthworks. Even settlements of a likely phase are not necessarily of the same period as "Celtic" fields now seen about them; thus, the fields near the Late Bronze Age settlement on Itford Hill, Sussex, were cultivated from some other settlement in the Romano-British period.[16] Integration of fields with any trackway leading into a settlement seems the best assurance of contemporary relationship, at least in some phase, though the individual fields might of course have suffered considerable subsequent alteration and not necessarily be characteristic of the period of the settlement.

Some of the following features are likely to be earlier, or later, or contemporary, as indicated, but this should be checked wherever possible.

(i) *Long barrows* exist which have been completely integrated in the pattern of later fields. Some are known to have been used as field sides (e.g. Bere Regis, Dorset, number 155 on O.S. map of Neolithic Wessex and R.C.H.M. Dorset, Volume II, forthcoming).

(ii) *Round barrows* are frequently found amongst "Celtic" fields but almost always at field corners or otherwise on the edges suggesting that they were there before the fields were laid out. Where there is a slope it is likely that a positive lynchet will lie against, or a little above, the uphill side of any barrow and a negative be found to have cut away below and beside it on the downhill side. This sometimes results in the barrow standing on a tongue representing the old ground surface. There is, however, growing evidence that

[16] VII Burstow and Holleyman 1957.

the first "Celtic" fields were already being tilled at in least the Middle Bronze Age (see p. 36), a period when many barrows were built, so it is possible that some barrows of this period may yet be found unambiguously lying on the *positive* lynchets of "Celtic" fields. The subsequent great pressure on arable land, notably in the Romano-British phase, nonetheless makes it possible that such instances might be masked by subsequent cultivation within a field pattern once more designed to respect the barrows and thus place them at the edges of the fields we see. (Such considerations make examination of the old ground surface under barrows a matter of particular interest.) It is ironic that the Deverel barrow (Milborne, Dorset), after which one element of the Bronze Age *Deverel-Rimbury* culture was named, lay at the corner of a "Celtic" field romantically described but not recognised by W. A. Miles, its excavator.[17] The field remains have since been so ploughed-down that it is now no longer possible to be absolutely sure whether the barrow was built on a positive lynchet or not but Miles' description and the poor vestiges on the ground suggest that it was indeed set a little way back from the top of a normal "staggered angle" (cf. p. 24) and thus later than at least the earliest phase of these fields.

A case in which air photographs suggested very strongly a relationship that work on the ground eventually disproved is shown on Plate IIA. Conjoined disc barrows and a single disc barrow of the Early Bronze Age seem to sprawl on top of "Celtic" field angles. This is an illusion. Careful field inspection[18] (independently confirmed by P. P. Rhodes' excavation) shows the uphill banks of the disc barrows buried under ancient ploughsoil, the plane of the natural slope on which the barrows were built being different from the artificial plough-altered slope of the "Celtic" fields beside them (Fig. 2E.) These barrows could have been easily levelled, so, quite apart from negative fear and respect, their preservation might in part be due to the positive close association between ritual ideas of rebirth and fertility and the processes of farming.

[17] W. A. Miles, *The Deverel Barrow* (1826), p. 17.
[18] By R.C.H.M., to whom I am also indebted for use of their plan.

Excavation might yet show plough furrows under a barrow in this country (cf. p. 36). So far the only evidence is for "slash-and-burn" methods of agriculture—to be associated with the temporary cultivation of cleared areas in scrubby woodland rather than with a system of settled farming.[19]

It should perhaps finally be mentioned that not all mounds are barrows, as Crawford proved when he dug one such on a lynchet only to find it contained no burial and covered Romano-British sherds in the old turf-line underneath it.[20]

(iii) *Isolated platforms or enclosures* too small for cultivation or settlement proper, their purpose probably varied, but perhaps in some cases stack areas, sometimes seen amongst fields away from settlements. Instances are known, for example, of triangular areas apparently set out by fencing off the corners of fields which, from the lynchets that have built up above the "triangles", seem to have continued in cultivation.[21]

(iv) *Ponds*. Though square ponds are probably all relatively modern, circular "dew ponds" might be very old even though their name is not.[22] A number of large ponds also have Saxon names[23] but the paucity of contemporary ponds in settlements suggests that most ponds amongst "Celtic" fields are in fact of later date and should always be regarded with suspicion unless clearly associated with a settlement.

(v) *Marl pits*. Pliny says that the ancient Britons used chalk to marl their fields, referring to pits 100 feet deep.[24] The practice is apparently substantiated, for example, by the finding of chalk fragments in a pre-Roman non-calcareous arable soil at Verulamium (St. Albans, Herts.)—but there is no archaeological evidence for

[19] At Lockington, Leicestershire, M. Poznansky, *T.L.A.S.*, XXXI (1955), p. 24.

[20] III Crawford 1924, p. 5.

[21] E.g. Little Bredy, Dorset, R.C.H.M. Dorset, Vol. II, forthcoming.

[22] "Dew" seems to be a misleading description first applied in the nineteenth century, but ponds on the high downland were objects of wonder to Gilbert White in 1776 (*Natural history of Selborne*, Lutterworth Ed., 1951, pp. 207–10.) See also E. A. Martin, *Dew Ponds* (undated, *c.* 1910).

[23] O. G. S. Crawford, *Archaeology in the Field* (1953), Chap. II and App. 2.

[24] I Pliny, Book XVII (4), 6 and 8.

contemporary pits more than about 12 feet deep (in settlements) in the area of surviving "Celtic" fields. It seems very likely that the chalk dug out during the construction of storage pits in settlements from the Late Bronze Age into the Romano-British period was used as such since most of these pits were eventually filled up with rubbish rather than the chalk that had come out of them. Otherwise any original marl-pits are difficult to identify since marling of this sort has gone on, probably, ever since, and the downs are sometimes covered in long, often regularly disposed lines of chalk pits, each pit often 30 to 50 or more feet across and several feet deep (cf. Plate IIA). Some were dug as late as this century and for an account of their use see R. Wightman, *My Homeward Road* (1950), p. 176. They are especially found where "clay-with-flint" lies on the chalk. One was excavated near Woodcuts by Pitt-Rivers.[25]

(vi) *Sunken tracks or hollow-ways* must be distinguished from so-called "covered ways". They are usually formed by the constant treading of many cattle along a climbing track, and their existence would therefore seem of economic significance. They are common on mediaeval routes. By contrast, "double-lynchet ways" and banked tracks integrated with "Celtic" fields are rarely hollowed. (cf. Frontispiece.) Great care should always therefore be taken to check whether an apparent relationship of hollow-way and "Celtic" fields or settlements is genuine.

"*Covered ways*" is a term used in older archaeological literature for what would now mostly be recognised as "cross-ridge-dykes" or "linear ditches", further discussed below.

(vii) *Cross-ridge dykes*. This term is used to describe earthworks which run across ridges but otherwise differ somewhat regionally. In Sussex for instance, they usually have ditches on the uphill side and these are often continued from either end by tracks leading through contemporary "Celtic" fields.[26] Wessex also has some of these but the more widespread form, not directly associated with tracks has its bank on the uphill, or dominant side. Occasionally,

---

[25] *Excavations in Cranborne Chase*, Vol. I, p. 4 and Pl. III, pit 66.
[26] E. C. Curwen, "Cross-ridge dykes in Sussex" in *Aspects of Archaeology in Britain and Beyond* (Ed. W. F. Grimes), Chap. VII.

they are found in pairs facing outwards with a settlement set between.[27] At other times, sufficiently often to suggest a contemporary association, they lie at some remove on the approach to a hillfort. If not purely defensive they are probably to be connected with the needs of enclosing stock, and when found actually amongst "Celtic" fields are likely therefore to be either later or earlier than that particular group. Even though the "Celtic" fields have been largely destroyed it might still be possible to establish the relationship without excavation. For example, since many lynchets athwart a slope are known to increase in height downhill any apparent increase in the height of a dyke as it runs down a slope will suggest that it has been built on a lynchet. The ditch in such a case is likely to be on the uphill side, that is, dug out from behind the head of the lynchet. (Fig. 5C.)

(viii) *Earthworks connected with the needs of pasture.* It is by no means certain that all pastoral farms would include any arable land but there is little doubt that all arable farmers kept stock and would therefore require pasture.

*Arable-pasture rotation.* It is highly desirable that stock should be folded on arable fields when fallow, and since settled farmland needs to lie idle at regular intervals to recover its capacity to yield good crops this will often have provided such pasture as was necessary. There will not, therefore, necessarily be any land clearly distinguishable as pasture in the sense of showing no signs of cultivation. How, then, in such cases were growing crops protected? The answer must lie either in the tethering of animals, in the employment of herdsmen (possibly on distant pasture) or in the use of enclosures.

It is probable that very many fields were not fenced (see the evidence of the section in Fig. 2C) but it is quite possible that some were used as pens, and it would be interesting to establish, for instance, how effective the stone walls around some fields really were. Perhaps they were reinforced by a "dead-hedge". If considerable stock were carried the division of the farmland into two blocks seems highly probable. Perhaps this explains the arrangements in Fig. 3A where a

[27] As on Knowle Hill, *Procs. D.F.C.*, 78, p. 74, and 79, pp. 106-7, and forthcoming.

## FIG. 5. POINTS OF RECOGNITION

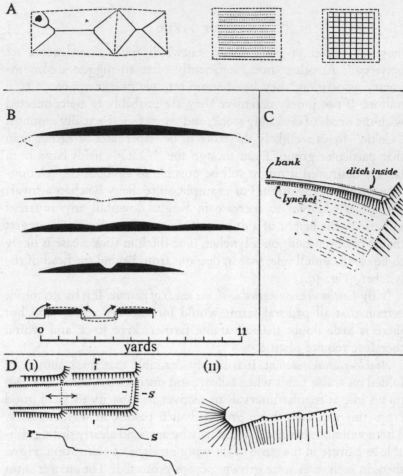

A. *Left:* Diagram of *round-and-round* ploughing or cropping marks showing diagonals and lines falsely suggesting an enclosure in the top left of the field, actually around an obstruction.
   *Middle:* Diagram of ridge ploughing (modern). Lines represent furrows and dots the ridge crests. Headlands at ends.
   *Right:* Diagram showing occasional effect of modern cross ploughing, known to have been mistaken for "Celtic" fields! (Cf. p. 39.)

B. Profiles of Ridges. In order from top:
   Broad plough-ridge (*broad rig*) on heavy land; medium development.
   Similar on chalk downland—approx. maximum development known to the writer.
   *Narrow-rig*
   Broad plough-ridge re-ploughed with a technique of narrow ridges.
   "Water-carriage" of water meadows.
   "Lazy-Beds". Arrows indicate how turves (black) are dug out and laid on original surface. (Cf. pp. 46–50.)

C. Diagram showing how a lynchet sometimes increases in height downhill. It is assumed here that a bank of uniform height has been built on the edge of the lynchet and merged with it. The apparent increase in the height of the bank is then due to the underlying lynchet. (Cf. p. 33.)

D. (i) Secondary ploughing amongst "Celtic" fields. The bank formerly dividing the lower fields has been ploughed over and new negative and positive lynchets created. A false effect of a bank has been caused at "S" by the heavy plough turning the soil against the slight slope assumed.
   (ii) A spur on which "Celtic" fields have been totally destroyed except for the tell-tale run of scarps at the edge.

bank and ditch running S.W. from a point near the west corner of
the enclosure undoubtedly divides fields that are laid off it on either
side. The bank and ditch running north to south, 500 feet east of
the enclosure, however, cuts across "Celtic" fields.[28] There are many
parallel instances elsewhere in Wessex. Such linear earthworks
usually consist of a single bank and V-shaped ditch which even when
dug out is rarely more than 5 feet below the bank. One excavated
example was palisaded.[29] Occasionally they form great enclosures,
sometimes around uncultivated ground.[30] They have been shown to
exist in the Late Bronze Age and Iron Age and there is little doubt
that some are Romano-British. The introduction of *spelt* as, probably,
a winter-sown crop in the Iron Age provided a likely new reason for
enclosure.

Small ditched enclosures—like the example used above—may have
been built as early as the Late Bronze Age and be directly associated
with fields or linear works but it is not always easy to give a date
for the more regular unassociated enclosures on downland. Some are
mediaeval.

## Farm boundaries

These may on occasion be marked by linear ditches but mostly
they are not. It is to be presumed that natural features such as
streams, very steep slopes, woodland and the like, as well as
"through roads" could serve the purpose, but when many hundreds
of acres lie together some other sort of boundary needs to be looked
for. A clue may lie in the possibility of recognising the "gates" into
fields. The absence of gates communicating from one set of fields
to another is a sure way of knowing when one has reached the bounds
of a modern farm. Assuming that the fields were not fenced or
walled and that the ploughs in use were as light as we believe them
to have been, there would be no necessity for gates on flat ground.

[28] "Fragments found all along the 300 ft. (i.e. which Pitt Rivers caused to be
excavated) were Bronze Age Pottery of No. 1 quality." (*Excavations in Cranborne
Chase*, Vol. IV, p. 190). Such evidence taken alone surely dates the fields it cuts
through rather than the ditch itself.
[29] *W.A.M.*, XLVI, pp. 450–2.
[30] Cf. VIII Hawkes 1939.

On any slope, however, experience would show that the situation alters, since lynchets are built up. These grow to become uncomfortable, if not impassable, barriers and that is, perhaps, why fields were occasionally arranged with "staggered angles". (See Fig. 4A.)

When a straight run of lynchets set end to end is met amongst fields whose angles are, otherwise, "staggered", it may be suggested that it marks a farm boundary. Plate III, Kingston, Corfe Castle, supports the suggestion. Here there appear to be two settlements, one to the east of a straight run of lynchets and another (mostly) to the west of the same run. A complex history, ending in the throwing-together of "Celtic" fields to accommodate a heavy plough (which has left its mark in *broad* and *narrow rig*, see p. 47), nonetheless suggests that in the original marking out of the ground a virtually straight boundary line divided two farms.

## DATING

The dating of "Celtic" fields will depend chiefly on a proper assessment of their relationship to settlements and other earthworks. The dating of objects from marking-out ditches or walls would be important. Pottery scattered on the fields with manure provides some guide but by no means an infallible one. If in some phases cattle were not folded, or if they were folded at some distance from the settlement away from the possibility of domestic rubbish being mixed up with manure, the surviving pottery would be incomplete testimony. In acid soils there is an opportunity to attempt dating by pollen analysis.

There are substantial grounds for thinking that some "Celtic" fields may have already existed in the Middle Bronze Age, if not earlier. The Continental evidence of plough furrows under barrows even of the Early Bronze Age had already suggested the possibility but now at Gwithian, in Cornwall, there is the extensive area of plough furrows excavated by Mr. Charles Thomas apparently belonging to rectangular fields whose lowest ploughed stratum may date to the last part of the Early Bronze Age (sixteenth century B.C.).[31]

[31] Information kindly given by Mr. Thomas. Cf. p. 9.

All that is lacking, so far, is a pattern of fields large enough to be recognisable as "Celtic" or not. In Wessex and Sussex, on the other hand, it is the vast growth of the "Celtic" field system, involving alteration as well as expansion which makes it both difficult to find the ancestral groups and to be sure of their original form if found.[32] Mediaeval and later ploughing further complicate the task. Since settlements of the Bronze Age earlier than its *late* phase are extremely rare the evidence of relationship with round barrows becomes crucial (see p. 30).

All evidence bearing on the extent of cultivation (particularly in relation to settlements) at any period is of importance. There must have been a very considerable spread of fields in the pre-Roman Iron Age, at least, but the remains which can be specifically given this label are regrettably few. In some cases this may be due to pottery of earlier periods in the lynchets being buried under plough soil containing pottery belonging to the latest phase of cultivation only.[33] Over the fields as a whole, however, away from the edges, there can scarcely be any stratification and the plough will have mixed up pottery of all phases—the poorer quality ware perhaps disintegrating in the process.

Undoubtedly the phase of maximum cultivation was in the Romano-British period. It would be of the greatest interest to know by how much this area was larger than in the preceding era, and also for how long the Romano-British fields were tilled before the new Saxon settlement pattern was generally adopted.

ON AIR PHOTOGRAPHS (see also Chapter V)

The interpretation of air photographs is well learned from walking the ground with actual air photographs in hand but this is best done after reading some of the excellent works cited in the Bibliography,

[32] The find of a hoard of ornaments, now regarded as of the Middle Bronze Age, just under the present surface of a "Celtic" field on Elcombe Down, Ebbesbourne Wake, Wilts. (*W.A.M.*, LIII, 1949, pp. 104–12) strongly suggests Middle Bronze Age or earlier origins.
[33] Cf. Streatley Warren, Berkshire, *B.A.J.*, 51 (1948–9), pp. 51–2.

Section XX, bearing in mind that the actual archaeological significance of the remains shown may in some cases require review in the light of more recent knowledge. The following points are therefore only offered as a further commentary.

While *shadow* marks are thrown north of a scarp falling away from the sun and *shine* marks ("highlights"), light in texture, are due to reflection from scarps facing the sun, banks and scarps that run in line with the sun's rays are all too often very difficult to pick up and should therefore be sought in the faintest of signs. Conversely, steep east-to-west ridges may cast deep enveloping shadows over their north-facing slopes. It is a sad fact that "Celtic" fields are often found here in profusion! This is only one reason for seeking as many different sets of air photographs as possible.

When photographed in dull conditions, rough ground in particular tends to be uninformative. Clues may lie in scrub attracted to positive lynchets (see Frontispiece) or, conversely, relative lack of growth on stony banks—but care should be taken not to be misled by paths cut in bracken or low undergrowth.

Since lynchets were often dug for the stones in them such grubbing may be significant if seen to be in lines or in pits disposed at regular intervals (corresponding with the spacing of the lynchets). They will be distinguishable from marl-pits (p. 31) not least by being dug into actual lynchets.

*Soil marks* on arable land may be misleading if there are local variations, e.g. patches of clay-with-flints on chalk. Accumulation of soil along the floors of gullies can falsely suggest boundaries or enclosures; a stereoscope would betray it—or a closely contoured map. When on chalk alone "Celtic" fields are sometimes defined by white lines edged on either side by black. This may be due to the modern plough exposing chalk at the core of a bank or lynchet and assumes that the positive element of ploughsoil is spread on either side, but in some instances a possibility of some of the dark lines being ditches should not be entirely ignored. (Crawford's photograph of Windmill Hill, Hampshire, is challenging on this as well as on other counts.[34])

[34] VIII Crawford 1924, Pl. II.

*Crop-marks* of ditched "Celtic" fields in, e.g., the Fens are, of course, not in doubt and there present a wonderful picture of what seems to be an exclusively Romano-British pattern. Very rarely, as in 1959, the typical dark lines above ditches may be transformed in the last stages of extreme drought into the light *parch marks* more normally associated with starved growth above wall footings and the like. Crop-marks are usually narrower than the ditches they mark.

*Modern plough patterns* can sometimes be confusing. (Cf. Fig. 5A.) In ridge ploughing it is usual to vary the direction on different occasions. The deep furrows of earlier ploughing are therefore sometimes seen crossing the latest ones at right angles, making a pattern of squares. This effect is characterised by thin lines, sharp angles and the fact that the furrows will in each case be parallel to one side of the field.

In round-and-round ploughing and cropping the diagonals can be particularly misleading when they butt against each other making large squares or diamonds. If an obstacle such as an earthwork in the middle of the field has to be avoided it is possible that the plough marks will be bowed around it, suggesting an enclosure. The best clues to identification lie in the run of the diagonals to the modern field corners and the central "spines" connecting the pairs of diagonals.

# CHAPTER IV

## Strip-lynchets and ridge-and-furrow

"*Strip lynchets*" is a confusing term but one made respectable by long use. It refers to fields invariably bounded by lynchets but actually means the fields themselves. To avoid confusion it will be proposed here to call the scarped sides of the fields (i.e. the lynchets) the "risers" and the arable area the "treads".

In Chapter I they were called "long, narrow, often prominent terraces". By definition they are always found on slopes but many were originally surrounded by other strip fields either flat or ridged belonging to the same system.

It is suggested that they be sub-divided into three types:

(1) *Contour*, i.e. very approximately following the contours. These provide the most prominent, even dramatic, examples, as in Plate IV.

(2) *Up-and-down*. These may well have had a much wider distribution than is now apparent since their remains are much slighter and therefore much more easily destroyed than the *contour* type.

(3) An *intermediate form* running diagonally up the slope.

They may all be distinguished from the "Celtic" long fields by:

(i) "*open*" *ends*, either (*a*) running out on to an unploughed area, (*b*) butting direct on to a headland or a block of similar fields (a "furlong") set at right-angles, (*c*) ending in ramps to another level.

(ii) *ends which, if closed are curved or drawn-out.*

The *contour* type, when forced to a termination by some natural feature such as a steep bulge in the hillside, will most often end with one of its sides curving to meet the other (Fig. 4C), but it may also be "drawn out" in a strip only a few feet wide until it vanishes (cf. Plate IV).

(iii) *attenuated proportions*: in length they often approximate to 200 yards but their widths are very varied and depend to a marked degree on the slope of the ground. Examples 3 or 4 yards wide and as much as 50 times as long are not uncommon.

(iv) *an arrangement in parcels otherwise called "furlongs", "flats" or "falls".* Where the slope allows these may be set at right-angles to each other and be obvious.[1] When in runs of much more than 200 yards end to end along the contour furlong junctions might be marked by ramps.[2]

*A notable but rare exception* to the above is provided by some lyncheted strip fields on Dartmoor which, though apparently mediaeval, do not fit this description. They have squared ends and, though long, do not have the extreme proportions of normal strip lynchets. Nonetheless, they are arranged in parcels after the mediaeval fashion and it is this regular disposition over a large area which would appear above all to distinguish them from the "Celtic" long fields.[3]

*Marking out.* Strip lynchets, like "Celtic" fields, must have been marked out originally, in however rudimentary a fashion. In the case of steep or otherwise difficult slopes the method may have been linked to some preparation of the ground for ploughing (see below). Markers, "mere" or "bound" stones or posts, have sometimes survived to be found at the end of "flat" strip fields. Baulks or banks are still to be seen dividing strip fields in Dorset and where these are on a slope there is a measure of lynchet formation.[4] Such divisions show, however, what has recently existed and need not necessarily indicate an original method of demarcation. It should be noted that even though there are side banks the fields do not have banks across their ends.

*Status and size.* It cannot be assumed automatically that individual

[1] E.g. in Dorset, Bincombe or Knitson (Langton Matravers).

[2] E.g. Winterborne Steepleton. These examples will be published in R.C.H.M. Dorset, Vol. II.

[3] IX Shorter 1938.

[4] C. D. Drew, *A.,* XXII (1948), pp. 79–81, describes this happening in the surviving strips of the Isle of Portland. There are other examples, but now and for many years pasture, notably at Kingston, Corfe Castle. (R.C.H.M., Dorset. Vol. II, forthcoming.)

*strip lynchets* (any more than plough-ridges), especially when very narrow, represent full strip holdings. Conversely, although their length as found is frequently close to the statutory furlong, the mediaeval concept of "acre" tended to be quite unmathematical and, to quote F. W. Maitland, "a plot will be, and rightly may be, called an acre though its size is not that of any ideal acre".[5] Quite apart from this, regional variation in the size of perch and acre always needs to be considered.

*Structure.* It seems likely that the risers of most *strip lynchets* were built up in much the same way as the lynchets of "Celtic" fields—with the important difference that the vast bulk of them would have been accelerated in their formation by the use of a heavy plough always turning the slice downhill—certainly until the treads were flat enough to allow ridge ploughing. Reasonable proof of this gradual build-up is seen in a downward cross-slope of the treads. Occasionally the risers of contour *strip lynchets* are very high— 10 feet is by no means abnormal—and this means that much land is lost to the plough even though it could perhaps be grazed when the fields were lying fallow. It may be that observation of this development was in some instances responsible for the *up-and-down* layout, for the risers then grow on a secondary and much less steep slope. There is a limit, however, to the slope that could be ploughed in this latter fashion and the steepest known to the writer is 17 degrees and even here the headlands were on more gentle gradients.

Why some positive lynchets should build up and others tumble over the "negative" probably depends to some extent on the ploughman's willingness or otherwise to go right to the edge of his field, as well as on the possible existence of a bank or the like. In a flight of a number of treads and risers ploughing to the limits of each strip might therefore, in an extreme instance, ultimately cause soil from the top tread to reach the bottom one! This is perhaps an exaggerated concept but it has a bearing on the balance of positive and negative elements in the risers and provides one reason why the original slope of the hillside cannot safely be reconstructed by drawing a line through the middle point of each scarp face but only

[5] *Domesday and Beyond* (Collins, Fontana Ed., 1960), p. 442.

when it is actually found—either as an old turf line under the lynchets or visible as unploughed ground between terraces.

The possibility of some initial construction also has to be borne in mind. It is always tempting to consider this when flat treads are found but these might also, presumably, be the result of a very long period of ploughing. When they are spaced with a steep natural surface unploughed between the risers there is more initial reason for doubt. That deliberate levelling of obstructions took place is demonstrated by the recent discovery of a filled in Romano-British ditch under strip lynchets in north Wiltshire[6] and investigation of a series in Dorset has shown natural outcrop less than a foot under the head of a riser 7 feet high. Since it could scarcely, therefore, have been produced solely by plough action—either negative or positive—it is suggested that the terrace, at this particular point at least, was first levelled by digging.[7]

It will often be found that the risers decrease in height and the treads in width towards the ends of individual "contour" strip lynchets. The reasons for this are not clear to the writer—presumably one explanation would relate to anticipation of the turn and another to the shape of the hill-slope—but are well worth consideration.

*Relationships.* Strip lynchets often lie close to *nucleated settlements.* They are also found in areas beyond the recorded bounds of the open fields and instances are even known where they lie across the present-day *parish boundaries.*[8] Where this is not due to some modern alteration in the parish boundary it may result from a much older manorial arrangement antedating the creation of the ecclesiastical parish. It is a highly interesting subject for very careful individual investigation.

Very frequently contour strip lynchets are found clinging round the slopes under *hillforts* and sometimes can even be seen intermingled with the defences.[9] At Blewburton, Berkshire, they lie over

[6] V Wood and Whittington 1959.

[7] Bincombe, R.C.H.M. Dorset, Vol. II, forthcoming.

[8] E.g. Bishopstrow/Warminster and Bishopstrow/Norton Bavant: O.S. 6 inch map, Wilts. LII, N.W.

[9] E.g. Battlesbury, Warminster, Wilts.; Chalbury, Bincombe, Dorset; St. Catherine's Hill, Winchester, Hants.; Hinton Hill, Glos.

parts of a hillfort.[10] They are never contemporary and the reason for this frequent association most often seems to derive from the fact that hillforts tend to be on sites hanging over river valleys in which the later settlers found themselves short of suitable arable land and had to climb the valley sides to find it.

In all known instances of contact with *"Celtic" fields* the *strip lynchets* are later. They may run into a group of fields which have been levelled for them, slash over them crudely so that "Celtic" field angles and sides can be seen unconformably under the treads or projecting below the superimposed risers, or be more subtly incorporate as already described (p. 20 and Plate IV).

*Dating. Maps*—estate, enclosure and tithe—give innumerable instances of strip lynchets cultivated as strip fields often as late as the nineteenth century. Especial sharpness of profile or *narrow rig* (see below) may suggest such a relatively recent usage even when the cartographical evidence is absent. The real problem is, however, to establish when they were first introduced.

There is little doubt that elongated fields—the "Celtic" long fields—were in use at least in the Romano-British period[11] but no *strip lynchets* as defined here have yet been proved to originate as early as this. If they are ever found in Roman context it seems most likely that it will be near a Roman villa or town, the likely source of advanced techniques and certainly of some heavy ploughs. A survey just completed[12] of the "Celtic" fields which lie in rare proximity to a Roman villa at Brading, Isle of Wight, shows, however, no sign whatsoever of *strip lynchets* or ridge-and-furrow.

Assuming that they are post-Roman it is still debatable when strip lynchets began. The vast majority surely represent but one form of the strips of open-fields and documentary evidence, though sparse,

[10] V Collins 1952.

[11] And communal ploughing in long strips (*c.* 10 × 1) in the tenth century A.D. is attested by the Ancient Laws of Wales. See, e.g. J. E. Lloyd, *History of Wales* (1939), Vol. I, pp. 294–6.

[12] By A. Aberg and the writer on behalf of the British Association Research Committee on Ancient Fields. The use of a heavy fixed mould-board plough at Brading is indicated by a winged ploughshare—and corn production in the late Roman period by a T-shaped corn-drying oven.

shows that a communal system of agriculture was practised in Wessex certainly by the end of the seventh century.[13] The more awkwardly situated strip lynchets might suggest the operation of land hunger— and perhaps a relatively late date—so it is always worth considering the local availability of other land.

*Distribution* is a factor worth considering both nationally and more locally. No statement of distribution covering the whole country is available[14] but some points may be made. They are found from Cornwall to Scotland. North of the Jurassic Way (roughly Axminster to Lincoln) "Celtic" fields appear to be an introduction of the Roman period and so strip lynchets there are with fair certainty later. In the lowlands of Scotland, indeed, a date as late as the seventeenth century has been suggested.[15]

Why strip lynchets are apparently absent or poorly represented in some areas where they might be expected is a matter for close local study, first of all to see whether widespread destruction, possibly encouraged by the existence of an easily destroyed type, e.g. up-and-down, might not be responsible.

Strip lynchets are frequently found immediately around nucleated settlements. (Occasionally, the former existence of a strip system will be apparent in the pattern of enclosure which to some extent "fossilises" the old arrangements.) But they are also found at some distance. Two factors have to be borne in mind: the ebb and flow of cultivation whereby the in-field was sometimes extended well beyond the bounds recognised on late maps, and the possible existence of blocks isolated from the "in-field".

The widespread occurrence of outlying strip systems is a fact in the south of England as well as the north. Every attempt should be made to date them archaeologically by assessing their relationship with other features but it has to be remembered that digging will not necessarily produce sherds of contemporary pottery, presumably because any manure was obtained from folds rather than

[13] Laws of Ine, *Cap.* 42.
[14] Dr. G. Whittington's thesis on *strip lynchets* in the south of England considers distribution there. (Unpublished; Reading University.)
[15] XVI Graham 1938.

middens.[16] Since not infrequently laid out over "Celtic" fields, a thin scatter of pottery derived from these earlier remains might indeed be found. Nevertheless, an excellent recent study shows how worthwhile in terms of dating and structure the excavation of strip lynchets can be.[17]

Though approximate dating is possible by archaeological means the organisation and tenurial implications cannot be worked out solely from the fields themselves and require some evidence from documents. Mediaeval extents may be of particular value in this context. Saxon charters also demand consultation whenever available (and are of most use after a full archaeological survey has been made) but it must be warned that "hlinc" will not necessarily mean an arable lynchet.[18] The use of documents is best seen by consulting the historical studies quoted in the bibliography, beginning perhaps with H. L. Gray.

### Ridge and furrow (Fig. 5B)

It is probably more difficult to generalise about types of ridge-and-furrow than about any other form of field remains. It is literally true that where it is found the only safe immediate assumption is that when last ploughed that particular area was gathered into ridges by a mould-board plough! In many instances, however, it certainly preserves an old pattern and in wet lands where it might be of vital importance to drainage it could only be safely done away with if other provisions were made for taking away the water.

Before considering distinctive *types* it is perhaps worth mentioning three other forms of ridge which might confuse in one way or another. *Water-meadow ridges*, or "water-carriages", well known in large areas of Wessex, look like and, indeed, were usually built up in the same way as, broad ridge-and-furrow but are usually distinguishable by water channels running centrally along their backs

[16] Cf. *Sx. A.C.*, 97 (1959), p. 110, where mediaeval custumals are quoted which lay down careful regulations for manuring.

[17] V Wood and Whittington 1959.

[18] For a valuable note on Saxon Charter terminology and open fields, see *V.C.H.*, Wilts., II (1955), p. 13, footnote 65.

and by the presence of immediately adjacent "feeder" channels.[19] A curious form of *very broad ridge*, 40 yards or more wide, found in long runs amongst old open-fields on the river gravels, is best explained as a track or occupation way.[20] *Lazy beds*, on the other hand, are arable but spade-built ridges, usually 2 feet to 8 feet wide divided by furrows 1 foot to 3 feet wide, now generally confined to Ireland, the Hebrides and the Faroes, but which might explain certain Roman remains found in this country and are probably cognate with prehistoric and Viking ridges discovered in Scandinavia and Holland.[21]

*The formation of ridge-and-furrow* has already been explained (p. 10) and is not in doubt but it is worth attempting sub-division on the basis of size and pattern.

*Narrow rig* (Plate IIB and Fig. 5B) is a term used by the writer to describe a form of ridge-and-furrow which occurs in a demonstrably late context at least in southern England, Shropshire and parts of Wales. Five yards or less in width it is almost always straight and low. It is found on all soils and in all situations—in enclosed fields and on open downland, on "Celtic" fields and on *strip lynchets* and even on earlier *broad rig*, sometimes producing an odd fluted pattern not to be confused with the "green furrows" (intermediate narrow grass ridges between broad ridges) sometimes found in the Midlands.[22] Its overall distribution is patchy but it seems to occur in many parts of Britain in the late eighteenth century and nineteenth century, though there are references to narrow "stitches" at a much earlier date.[23]

*Broad rig* (Fig. 5B) is, equally arbitrarily, wider than 5 yards. It may be low, as is common on chalk country, or so well developed, in the heavy clay lands, as to warrant the term "high-back". It may be quite

[19] Cf. *W.A.M.*, LV (1953), pp. 105–18.

[20] XIV R.C.H.M. 1960, p. 32.

[21] E. Estyn Evans, *Irish Folk Ways*, 1957, Chap. XI. J. G. D. Clark described as "lazybeds" a series of short prominent ridges in the Romano-British settlement at Cottenham, Cambs. (XIII Clark 1949.) Cf. also IV Steensberg 1960.

[22] V Orwins 1954, p. 46. Note that there are numerous instances of strips in the open fields being ley. Cf. Beresford in *Y.A.J.* (1950), p. 334, or Hoskins (Ed.) *Studies in Leicestershire Agrarian History*, p. 136.

[23] E.g. William of Folkingham, *Feudigraphia* (1610), p. 48.

straight or sinuous, usually in the shape of a reversed "S". It has been argued that this form was the product of the technique of turning a long plough-team and is therefore relatively early.[24] Broad rig survived side by side with narrow rig but by and large seems to be the early form and thus is often found in typically open-field patterns of "furlongs". In such a situation headlands are invariably found. One consequence of this is that if a block of rig runs right up to a hedge or wall it must originally have run on beyond and thus antedate the enclosure. Rarely, on the open downland, instances are known where it ends on earlier lynchet edges without any headland. Here a "knuckled" effect may be observed where the turning plough has thrown soil to leave bulges at the end of each ridge on the head and face of the old lynchet.

Since a slice cannot be turned against any considerable gradient and, indeed, because of the needs of drainage, on any slope of more than a few degrees the rig will run up-and-down hill (slopes of 17 degrees being known). On gentle slopes, however, the rig may lie contour-wise and the effects of gravity will then tend to displace the crowns of the ridges. An effect very similar to that of shallow rounded, strip lynchets will then be produced but consideration will make it clear that there is no unploughed scarp. For the sake of brevity only it could be called "lynchetted rig".

*Dating.* Some considerations have already been given. Comparison with detailed estate maps which show every strip will always produce interesting results—the nature of which it is not the purpose of this booklet to forecast—but a telling comparison between ground and map is illustrated, for instance, by W. R. Mead for the parish of Soulbury, Buckinghamshire.[25] Here, the old furlongs were still identified as blocks of ridge-and-furrow correctly aligned, but the numbers of actual ridges scarcely tallied with the eighteenth-century strip holdings.

Downland *broad rig* (Plate V) is known to be widespread particularly in Wiltshire, but occurs also in Dorset, Hampshire, Berkshire and, probably, Sussex, while William Marshall in 1780 had noted

---

[24] VI Eyre 1955. E. Kerridge, *Econ. Hist. R.*, 4 (1951–2), p. 34, prefers to say "more old-fashioned".        [25] VI Mead 1954.

"high ridges" even on the "thin light chalky loam" of the Yorkshire Wolds.[26] In such relatively remote situations there are no nucleated settlements to suggest its date but very often the remains of farms of much earlier periods!

On its own account, therefore, like the more remote strip lynchets with which it is sometimes found associated, this downland broad rig presents a considerable challenge to be dated and attributed. While the vast bulk, at least, is with little doubt post-Roman every case should be considered separately and if possible related to a document. Excavation, except to establish a relationship or to look for datable objects which might be significant, is pointless, and William Marshall himself noted that in section there was little to distinguish the ridges from natural formations.[27]

The Roman plough could have built up rig but to leave permanent ridges requires a definite policy which is characteristically mediaeval and later. It can scarcely have been needed for drainage on the downland and would seem therefore to reflect the habits built up by cultivation of the valleys below.

Quite apart from the dating problem it is important because it stresses the usages to which the downland has been put since the Roman period and, since its slight form is sometimes difficult to detect, it can lead to much misunderstanding if overlooked. When laid over "Celtic" fields, for instance, it tends to be confined by the higher lynchets but to ignore the lesser and to produce, occasionally, a misleading appearance of "Celtic" strip fields. A number of examples has been published but the true nature of the remains not always recognised (see, e.g., Plate V). Thus while in 1935 Dr. Crawford wrote about the remarkable "superimposed cultivation systems" of the type in question on Thornham Down, Wiltshire, cognate remains are not always described as such in his earlier, pioneer works.[28]

It should be noted that much of the downland broad rig is not

[26] On the Yorkshire Wolds *in-field/out-field* was apparently practised until the Napoleonic Wars (VI Kerridge 1951, p. 25, citing the report of 1812).

[27] *Rural Economy of Gloucestershire* (1789), Vol. I, p. 81.

[28] See Bibliography, end of Section VI.

arranged in "furlongs" and, indeed, in the example quoted on Thornham Down the rig is of great length, and is unusual but not unique in that it not only lies diagonally across "Celtic" fields but also crosses the parish boundary.

Tenurial details, again, cannot with any certainty be derived from the fields themselves but if some examples can be worked out with the aid of documents and, perhaps, archaeological dating evidence then there will at least be analogies to consider. Finally, lest there be any misunderstanding, *run-rig* applies to the organisation of cultivation and not to the plough rig itself.[29]

[29] Cf. V Gray 1915.

# CHAPTER V

## Recording

THE foregoing elementary analysis of field remains is meant for the fieldworker—not least to encourage new fieldworkers—and every time any statement in it is independently confirmed—or shown to need qualification—then it has served its purpose.

Work on ancient fields requires above all to be undertaken with definite questions in mind. (Others are soon added!) General problems are touched upon in Chapter I and specific subjects for research suggested in Appendix I. These wider problems have to be formulated in local terms—such as, for instance: Are the remains all of one phase or period? Do they bear evidence of destruction which affects their value as evidence? Is there any sign of a settlement or farm boundary? Can barrows in the area be related to the field remains? Can field remains suggestively mediaeval be linked to any documentary reference? and so on. A proper understanding of processes and possibilities will answer more questions without excavation than in most branches of archaeology but, conversely, one of the purposes of fieldwork should be to show where and how excavation can answer what is then left unsolved.

It is highly desirable that the *same* questions are asked every time a survey is made. It is often just as important to have definite statements that certain features did *not* exist as that they did exist. Thus *tally cards* which embody the right questions can be of great help. Examples for "Celtic" fields and *strip lynchets* and ridge-and-furrow appear at the end of this section.

Assuming that a region of some size is under consideration a *distributional study* is an obvious first step and important on its own account. (Not least it will immediately impress the urgency of the threat to the fields.)

The information aimed at will include:

Limits of areas covered and preliminary assessment of the nature of the remains.

Location of settlements.

Location of well-preserved remains.

Location of other specific features of particular interest, e.g. field/barrow relationships, downland strip fields, *strip lynchet*/"Celtic" field junctions, field types, possible farm boundaries.

Foreseeable threats to the remains.

This will provide the basis for priorities in further work and if resources and time are limited and the remains perhaps scrappy it may be that a concentration on some specific feature such as mentioned above would make the most valuable practical contribution.

But it is also the stage at which action can be taken to preserve the most important features, at least until fuller investigation has been made. This is a matter best tackled through the local archaeological society but it should be remembered that many farmers, if they and their land are treated with consideration, are sympathetic to reasonable pleas.

When well-preserved groups are found they require planning. Indeed, every opportunity should be taken to make a plan provided that destruction has not gone too far. Each line drawn is literally the answer to some question of fact or interpretation and is liable suddenly to illumine one's understanding of the whole site. The result is also a precise statement that can be used as the basis for any further consideration.

Since large areas are sometimes involved it is normally necessary to confine plans to a scale of 6 inches to the mile, the most convenient for transcription from air photographs. As this is sometimes too small to show clearly the nature of relationships or even of very small fields, and since it is always inadequate for the proper portrayal of settlements, a reasonable presentation can be allowed to consist of a *distribution map* drawn at a scale not less than $\frac{1}{2}$ inch to the mile, an *area plan* drawn at a scale not less than 6 inches to the mile showing the body of the fields and the position of settlements, and *detailed plans* of settlements and other features drawn at a scale of not less than 25 inches and, preferably, 50 inches or more, to the mile.

*Doing the work*

The preliminary list of sites is best compiled first from secondary sources and then added to by examining air photographs and the ground. Modern O.S. 1 inch outline (black-and-white) maps form excellent backgrounds for marking on these sites tentatively in coloured pencil.

The Archaeological Branch of the Ordnance Survey hold invaluable series of annotated maps and index cards which are available for inspection at their headquarters at Chessington, Surrey. Otherwise, the county or other local archaeological society and its museum and library and the county library are the points of departure.

Many counties have had bibliographies prepared. Several have "histories" written in the sixteenth or seventeenth centuries and most have had "histories" written in the eighteenth or nineteenth centuries.

*The older O.S. maps* are also very important. The first 1 inch to 1 mile O.S. maps, for instance, date from the first decade of the nineteenth century and show earthworks then recognised. Photostats of the 2-inch and 3-inch scale drawings made for this survey are held in the Map Room of the British Museum. Contemporary field boundaries are shown. Working outwards from such sources an initial distribution at least of likely settlement areas can be made.

*Air photographs* are the most important of all aids and it is quite impossible to have too many of them. Virtually every photograph is liable to contribute something new to the understanding of an archaeological site. Broadly speaking, there are two main types: *vertical and oblique*. Vertical air photographs enable preliminary plans to be made for checking and adding to on the ground. R.A.F. prints at a scale of about 1 : 10,000, roughly 6 inches to the mile, are available for most of the country. They may be bought from the Air Ministry (S4 (e)) but enquiries should first be addressed to the Council for British Archaeology, 10 Bolton Gardens, S.W.5. Prints may be consulted (and, e.g., selections made for ordering) at the Air Photographs Library of the Ministry of Housing and Local Government, Whitehall, S.W.1. It is again necessary that an introduction should be effected and the Council for British Archaeology should be approached for this. They are convenient for transcription to Ordnance Survey 6-inch maps and, perhaps even more important, exist in long runs wherein each photograph in a run overlaps its neighbour by some 60 per cent. This means that they can (and should) be viewed stereoscopically, banks and lynchets then standing in relief and "flat" dark marks such as that made by modern traffic readily identified as such. Perfectly adequate *stereoscopes* can be bought for around 30 shillings through optical instrument dealers.

*Using these instruments* is simple though usually requires a little experimentation before the knack of obtaining an immediate three-dimensional effect is obtained. The photographs should be placed with shadows toward the viewer, corresponding points on an adjacent pair placed under each lens and the prints gently adjusted until the whole view springs into relief as a single picture. The process is described in detail by J. S. P. Bradford, in *Ancient Landscapes* (1957).

*Some notes on interpretation* have already been given (p. 37).

*The process of transcription* is not, however, easy since the scale is rarely quite the same as that of the maps and—worse—is not usually constant on the air photograph itself. It must be accepted, however, that in most cases and without very expensive apparatus the 6-inch scale plans can be only approximately accurate and this, for the area plans, is good enough if the most important sections are isolated for a full ground survey and careful descriptions are also written.

*Techniques of transcription.* If the air photograph scales are in fact constant and close to that of the map then virtually direct traces can be made, but however this is done any marking of the air photograph must be avoided, e.g. by covering it with a sheet of talc. Otherwise, since photogrammetric techniques are sometimes complex and best understood when set out in illustrated detail, only two methods, one "rough-and-ready" and another mechanical, are discussed below. As most ancient fields will not be far distant from modern features shown on air photograph and map, *proportional dividers* set in turn to the vertical and horizontal scales can be used to triangulate. If such instruments (which cost about £4) are not available ordinary dividers can be used and a simple proportional calculation made each time to adjust from photograph to map scale. In either case care must be taken not to mark the photographs with the divider points.

*Simple transcribing machines* (whose use is nonetheless an art rather than a science)—anharmonic rectifiers usually called "sketchmasters" —are in fact made. Some cost over £100 new but one version described by Trorey[1] could probably be made for much less. The principle of operation depends on being able to see the image of the air photograph "floating" over that of the map. Distortion in the photograph is corrected by canting it on a platform which can be tipped in any direction while the effect of superimposition is obtained by viewing map and air photograph together through a prism or the equivalent. When using this method of transcription it is sometimes necessary to outline the archaeological features on the photograph with fine lines drawn by a wax pencil. These can be easily removed later with a soft cloth. (*Note*: Whatever method is used it may be desirable to make a trace of the modern detail from the map and transcribe to that if lettering or conventional signs deface the map itself.)

*Oblique air photographs* are generally easier to interpret on first sight than vertical air photographs and since very many have been taken specially for archaeological purposes from a low level under the most favourable conditions of crop or light they are of the greatest use in providing detail information—often of sites revealed for the first time.

The late Dr. O. G. S. Crawford, the pioneer of archaeological aerial photography in this country, published many (as well as some very valuable near-verticals) and others are held by the Archaeological Branch of the Ordnance Survey at Chessington.

Major G. W. G. Allen took a large number of excellent air photographs in the 1930's, particularly valuable because they also preceded the wartime extension of ploughing, gravel-quarrying and the like. A catalogue of an exhibition of some of these, which are all in the care of the Ashmolean Museum at Oxford, illustrates their scope.[2]

[1] XX Trorey 1950, pp. 111–13.
[2] XX Harden 1948.

Dr. J. K. S. St. Joseph is still adding to the largest extant collection, held by the Cambridge University Committee for Aerial Photography. Plates IV and V indicate the great value of these photographs while the published catalogues give details of every photograph taken within the years they cover. (See Bibliography Sec. XX.)

Once sites have been identified and plotted a further check on any available maps or documents to throw light on mediaeval and later usage should help in the interpretation of the field remains. *Estate maps* and *enclosure maps*, almost always on a large scale, accurate and detailed, can be very useful. The County record office, or, in rare cases, the County Archaeological Society is likely to hold most of the enclosure maps but a great number of estate maps still remains in private hands. *Tithe maps*, most of which were made in the years immediately following the Tithe Commutation Act of 1836, also give detailed information and specify, in their attached awards, the names of fields (sometimes very suggestive) and indicate whether they were arable, pasture or meadow at the time. All the tithe maps for a given diocese should be found in the Diocesan Registry, if they have not been transferred to the County Record Office. Copies are sometimes held by rectors and vicars for their own parishes, but in any event all can be consulted at the Tithe Redemption Commission headquarters at 33 Finsbury Square, London, E.C.2. Enquiry should be made in advance. Bona fide students are not normally required to pay a search fee. Since tracing of maps is not allowed by the Tithe Commission it is only wise to take 6-inch O.S. maps to annotate.

*Geological drift maps* are also most important. Some areas are covered by published 1 inch to 1 mile sheets but the most useful, at a 6 inch to 1 mile scale (though not available for the whole country) can be consulted in manuscript form at the library of the Geological Survey in the Geological Museum, Exhibition Road, S.W.7. When related to the field plans they will clearly show, for instance, whether "Celtic" fields avoid (as they often do not) such heavy downland soils as is represented by "clay-with-flints".

*Documents* of mediaeval date are vastly too complex to be considered here. Attention can again only be directed to how they have been used in local studies by such historians as Hoskins and Finberg[3] and Beresford.[4]

*Ground checking and survey* come last of all and are the most vital part of the work, first, because some questions can only be answered by ground examination and, second, because the fields themselves will by and large soon be utterly destroyed. Records made now will be the vital evidence depended upon in the near future.

Work should be begun on those remains which are best preserved or conversely, whatever their present state, are under most imminent threat of destruction. Groups of "Celtic" fields in a really good condition apparently untouched by secondary cultivation are extremely rare—probably much more so than is generally realised—and it is above all worth while searching these out and investigating them thoroughly. Not least, acquaintance with these should make it easier to appreciate the significance of the more fragmentary remains elsewhere.

*Basic equipment*, in order of importance, for making area plans, includes:

1. 6 inch O.S. map or trace from it, with field remains transcribed in thin pencil lines, mounted on a rigid board.
2. Air photographs.
3. Pencils, including two in colour and one wax, pen, rubber and sharpener for pencils.
4. Hardwood scale calibrated at 6 inches to the mile. (6 inch long, costs about 5s.)
5. Hard-covered notebook.
6. 100-foot tape-measure.
7. 4-foot-long gardeners' canes.
8. Clinometer, whether balance-type or "Abney" level.
9. Magnetic compass.
10. Protractor (rectangular, not semi-circular type).
11. Cross-head and staff.
12. Camera.
13. Stout paper bags for small finds.

[3] E.g. H. P. R. Finberg and W. G. Hoskins, *Devonshire Studies*, and W. G. Hoskins, *Local History in England* (1959).
[4] E.g. *History on the ground* (1957).

An accurate and full transcription could be checked by using the first four items only. It is indeed necessary to rely so far as possible on the plan made from the air photographs for this small-scale work. Where slopes are not steep pacing should be adequate to verify distances and with experience it is possible to judge whether angles are sufficiently accurate so as not to require revision. The plain lines of the transcription when checked should be hachured with conventional short hachures of uniform length (cf. Fig. 3), to show the direction of fall in the scarps and at the same time indicate that they have been checked. It is impracticable to draw the hachures to scale. Banks can be indicated by barring the lines in fishbone fashion or merely by firming them in. Very faint remains or those accepted on the basis of air photographs only can be drawn as broken lines.

Only rarely, however, will perfection of interpretation and transcription be achieved and some alterations and additions must be expected. These must be drawn when on the ground and not from "booked" measurements. On steep slopes a tape should be used, held horizontally and measurements taken in a series of short runs if necessary. The gardeners' canes are used to sight through on a straight line from which offsets can be measured if necessary. A magnetic compass, preferably of the liquid type, can be used to plot new features and check angles but in this case it is necessary to draw a line representing magnetic north on the map. (The current magnetic variation can be worked out from the data given in the margin of the 1 inch O.S. map for the area and it is near enough to accept the sheet line at the edge of the 6 inch map as representing true north.) A cross-head for sighting angles at intervals of 45 degrees can be of great assistance.[5] These instruments can sometimes be bought second-hand though with ingenuity it should not be too difficult to improvise a substitute. (The Roman surveyors' "groma" might give a lead!)[6]

The plan will also require annotation (cf. Fig. 4A) and for this pencils cannot be too sharp or work too neat. Field slopes of more than about 12 degrees should be checked by clinometer and marked

[5] XX Atkinson 1953 describes this and other simple instruments such as the Abney level (clinometer).

[6] See, e.g. M. and C. H. B. Quennell, *Everyday Life in Roman Britain* (1937), p. 20.

on the plan beside a single-barbed arrow to indicate the direction of the fall. Adjacent untilled slopes should also be recorded as a guide to show what was thought untillable or, alternatively, to require explanation if no steeper than the fields. Significant lynchet heights are worth noting with a figure under the hachures concerned. The position of finds can be noted in colour as can key letters drawing attention to points which cannot be drawn in telling detail at this scale. Double lynchet tracks should be marked as plain lines spaced correctly and labelled "DL".

Superimposed ridge-and-furrow can be dealt with differently, according to type. *Narrow rig* of eighteenth- and nineteenth-century origins can safely be shaded in as a block with, however, its bounds clearly indicated, since lynchets are likely to have been formed at the edges. The direction of the ploughing should be noted by a double-headed arrow.

*Broad rig* requires more careful treatment. The first aim will be to indicate its relation to the "Celtic" fields. The double-headed arrow again suffices to show it over-riding pre-existing banks or lynchets. The actual number of ridges and their position must also be indicated. On a 6 inch scale this can only be done conventionally, e.g. by using lines of dots.

*The recording of strip lynchets* when they are unassociated with earlier fields involves a slightly different technique. Hachuring at a 6 inch scale is often out of the question because the treads are so narrow. On the other hand extensive mapping must depend on initial transcription from air photographs. There are obviously many answers to this and perhaps the most important is to draw accurately measured profiles with clinometer and tape across parcels of strips wherever it is seen to be significant. This will show detail that is essential to an understanding of the nature of these terraces. They also lend themselves to photography and the results can be very useful as well as pleasing to look at.

Again it may be said that these 6 inch-scale plans based on air photographs but carefully checked, amended and added to by work on the ground and supported by large-scale plans of selected sites or detail, represent the only practicable and adequate way of surveying very large areas. They provide a general picture showing the relationship of settlements to fields and to each other on contoured modern map bases to which a variety of other information—the documented limits of open-fields, geological drift, present treatment, and the like—can be added as necessary. Adequate annotation and description based on some sort of tally card immeasurably increase their value. The equally important larger-scale drawings will vary from plans of settlements at not less than 1:2,500 (approximately 25 inches to the mile, which is the scale of the largest O.S. map normally available) to field sketches of such things as "staggered angles" and secondary lynchet formation. Photographs can be very useful for these as well as for more general views and for any lynchet section fortunately exposed. A scale should always be incorporated in the picture. It is probably best to leave the drawing of the main lines of settlements, etc., on the 6 inch plan until the large-scale survey has been done and they can then be transferred.

If air photographs have been bought specially for the survey they should be brought into the field held flat against a hard-board and protected under a sheet of talc. This—or the air photographs themselves—can be marked lightly with a wax pencil to show the position of something that might have been omitted from the transcription but can then be transcribed later with the assured knowledge of its appearance on the ground.

The plans, when made, can be sprayed with an artist's fixative to prevent blurring of the pencil lines. They should, however, be prepared for final form as soon as possible and it may be thought desirable to enlarge the original small-scale plans photographically before re-drawing for publication. Authority should be sought if the O.S. background is to be used.

Excavation, to which fieldwork will almost inevitably lead, is an art that requires considerable prior experience under a competent director.[7] It will certainly form a part of the research into most of the problems which the British Association Committee venture to suggest in the Appendix that follows, and it is fitting that this booklet should end by drawing attention to what we do *not* know.

[7] XX Atkinson 1953 gives a clear idea of the scope of knowledge required.

# APPENDIX A

*Urgent Problems*

THE most urgent and comprehensive problem is how to make an adequate record of all remains so that evidence shall not be lost without trace and an attempt can be made to preserve the most significant. The following selection of problems is put forward as a series of specific pointers to the general need and as an enticement to those who are considering research projects. The most important thing is to obtain evidence from a detailed study of the field remains while they still exist. This requires much time and care, often limiting investigations to specific sites, and is certainly worthy of the consideration of research students or of societies (who might thus qualify for a Carnegie grant through the Council for British Archaeology).

1. *The earliest fields*

(a) Are these the curvilinear plots, e.g. of north-eastern Yorkshire? What is the date and cultural attribution of these remains?

(b) Taking known Bronze Age settlements what is the demonstrable extent and original character of the attributed fields? Can their economy (in sandy areas) be further demonstrated by an examination of cultivation furrows and pollen horizons?

(c) What is the relationship of fields to Neolithic and Bronze Age barrows?

2. *Communications*

The existence of ancient fields often enables the system of roads to be reconstructed. How far does this communication system in a region throw light on the use of ridgeways as through roads, the existence of pasture at long remove from settlements, sources of water, and the extent and type of usage? E.g., How early can worn hollow-ways be dated?

3. *"Ranches"*

How do the linear ditches of Wessex relate to the keeping of stock and to "Celtic" fields? What settlements are they associated with? What is their dating span?

4. *Cross-dykes*

What is the function and dating span of the cross-dykes of "Sussex" type?

5. *A representative farm of a specific type in a particular period*

What was the pattern of its fields and their limit, and the nature of other features (pits, platforms and enclosures) that might exist away from the settlement amongst the fields? Where was its pasture? What was the relationship of livestock to arable activity? An attempt at this is badly needed in different regions, in chalk (where no hedges?) and in stone country where there were walls.

6. *"Celtic" long fields*
   Isolate and determine attribution.

7. *Roman villa fields*
   The Isle of Wight in particular has ancient fields immediately adjacent to villas.

8. *"Celtic" fields north of the Jurassic Way*
   What is their attribution?

9. *The possibility of Roman/Saxon continuity*
   Dr. Finberg has suggested a method of investigation without fields (at Withington) VIII Finberg 1955. Can an area be found *with* ancient fields?

10. *Strip-field systems (mostly broad ridge-and-furrow) on the high downland*
    What is their distribution, attribution and dating span?

11. *Strip lynchets*
    How early can these be dated?

12. *Strip lynchets*
    Can their method of layout be determined; is there any evidence for artificial structure; can the method of use, e.g. of very narrow treads without apparent room for a plough to turn, and the distribution in *furlongs* be determined?

13. *Saxon and early-mediaeval estate boundaries*
    These merit working out for their own sake but are particularly telling if they can be related to ancient field remains.

14. *Experiments*
    To guide current investigation, e.g. to provide data on lynchet formation, yields of primitive crops in varying circumstances, etc.

# APPENDIX B

*A Form of Tally Card for "Celtic" Fields*

1. *Classification* (note if signs of later interference or adaptation):
2. *Location:*
   - (a) Maps O.S. 6 inch (fields plotted direct on—sheet number therefore becomes index to plan)
   - (b) *Boundary points* with map references
3. *Total acreage:*
4. *Geology and Topography:*
   - (a) *Geology*—from maps and as noted on ground
   - (b) *Heights* above O.D.
   - (c) *Type of country* (note water)
   - (d) *Present treatment* of land (including wood), and *summary of condition*
   - (e) Any indication of *past treatment* (deal with any superimposed strip system in detail)
5. *Summary:*
   - (a) Any *settlement* (and see (6) below)
   - (b) Any *tracks, ponds, enclosures, mounds, ancient marlpits,* etc.
   - (c) Any possible *boundary*
   - (d) Any particular *grouping*
   - (e) Any particular *type* (note any marked constancy of size)
   - (f) *Area* of largest and smallest, and if any constant. (Does ground determine?)
   - (g) *Walls, banks or lynchets.* Lynchet heights if unusual. Do they increase in height downhill? Materials in. If walls, any sign of entrances?
   - (h) *Slopes* if unusually steep
   - (j) *Any other relationships,* e.g. of fields to each other or to other earthworks
   - (k) Any *finds* on ground
6. *Amplified descriptions:*
7. *Note on investigation* (detailed or rapid; extent of reliance on air photographs)
8. *References:*
   - (a) *Maps* other than 6-inch O.S. used—estate, tithe, etc.
   - (b) *Plans* made other than 6-inch scale
   - (c) Air *photographs* used
   - (d) *Ground photographs* taken
   - (e) *Bibliography*

*Date:*

# APPENDIX C

*A Form of Tally Card for Strip Fields*

1. *Classification:* strip lynchets (SL); broad rig (BR)—if divided by banks or balks (SB)
2. *Location:* Maps O.S. 6-inch. Boundary points with map references (8 figures)
3. *Situation:*
4. *Acreages:*
5. Whether they fit into a strip pattern on tithe or estate or enclosure maps; whether the fields on modern maps preserve a recognisable strip pattern round about.
6. *Conditions* (including note on any narrow rig and present treatment):
7. *Features:*
   - (a) Whether arranged in *furlongs* and how, detail of occupation ways and other boundaries
   - (b) Length (noting if full original extent or not), and shape in plan (noting if any reversed "S")
   - (c) Height of lynchets; whether natural ground surface appears between SL; nature of divisions otherwise (balk or bank, etc.)
   - (d) Width; does it vary? Areas of treads
   - (e) Slope along treads (if considerable)
   - (f) Slope across treads (if considerable)
   - (g) Form of strip heads: curved or "drawn-out"; run-out on to un-ploughed ground; headland (note butt junctions of furlongs), approach ramps; knuckled (if rig)
   - (h) Any structural features?
   - (i) Relationships to each other and other earthworks, including "Celtic" fields
8. *Amplified descriptions:*
9. *Nature of investigation* (detailed or rapid)
10. *References:*
    - (a) Cross-references
    - (b) Plans made
    - (c) Air photographs used
    - (d) Ground photographs taken
    - (e) Bibliography

*Date:*

# SELECT BIBLIOGRAPHY

NOTE.—The bibliography is divided into sections intended to help the reader towards further study rather than to correspond simply with the chapter headings. The Sections are:

    I Classical sources

    II Some early references to ancient fields in this country and to the origin of lynchets

    III The growth of modern recognition of different classes of fields and general studies on ancient agriculture

    IV Implements and farming practice

    V *Strip-lynchets, open fields* etc.

    VI Ridge-and-furrow, *open fields* etc.

VII-XIX Regions, sites and other countries

    XX Aerial photography; survey

References to the bibliography in the text give section, author and date. Thus "III Curwen 1932 (*a*)" is a reference to Dr. E. C. Curwen's article on "Ancient Cultivations" in *Antiquity*, Vol. VI (1932), pp. 389–406.

*List of Abbreviations*

| | | |
|---|---|---|
| A | = | *Antiquity* |
| A.H.R. | = | *The Agricultural History Review* |
| A.J. | = | *The Archaeological Journal* |
| A.N.L. | = | *The Archaeological News Letter* |
| A. of S. | = | *The Advancement of Science* |
| Ant. J. | = | *The Antiquaries Journal* |
| Arch. | = | *Archaeologia* |
| Arch. Camb. | = | *Archaeologia Cambrensis* |
| Arch. Cant. | = | *Archaeologia Cantiana* |
| B.A.J. | = | *The Berkshire Archaeological Journal* |
| C.B.A. | = | The Council for British Archaeology |
| D.A.J. | = | *The Derby Archaeological Journal* |
| D.F.C. | = | *The Proceedings of the Dorset Field Club* (or Natural History and Archaeological Society) |
| E.H.R. | = | *English Historical Review* |
| Econ. Hist. R. | = | *Economic History Review* |
| Geog. J. | = | *The Geographical Journal* |
| H.F.C.P. | = | *The Hampshire Field Club Proceedings* |
| J.R.S. | = | *The Journal of Roman Studies* |
| N.D.F.C.T. | = | *The Newbury and District Field Club Transactions* |

| O.S. | = | Ordnance Survey |
|---|---|---|
| Ox. | = | Oxoniensia |
| P.D.A.E.S. | = | Proceedings of the Devon Archaeological Exploration Society |
| P.P.S. | = | Proceedings of the Prehistoric Society |
| P.S.A.S. | = | Proceedings of the Society of Antiquaries of Scotland |
| R.C.A.M. (Scot.) | = | Royal Commission on Ancient Monuments, Scotland |
| R.C.A.M. (Wales) | = | Royal Commission on Ancient Monuments, Wales |
| R.C.H.M. | = | Royal Commission on Historical Monuments, England |
| Sx. A.C. | = | Sussex Archaeological Collections |
| Sy. A.C. | = | Surrey Archaeological Collections |
| T.L.A.S. | = | Transactions of the Leicestershire Archaeological Society |
| T.L.C.A.S. | = | Transactions of the Lancashire and Cheshire Antiquarian Society |
| U.B.S.S. | = | Proceedings of the University of Bristol Speleological Society |
| V.C.H. | = | Victoria County History |
| W.A.M. | = | Wiltshire Archaeological Magazine |
| Y.A.J. | = | The Yorkshire Archaeological Journal |

I. *CLASSICAL SOURCES.* Snippets on farming practice in Britain refer to marl pits, climate and harvesting, corn drying, storage and threshing but not, descriptively, to the fields themselves.

*Useful summaries* with references in:

E. C. Curwen: *Sx. AC.*, LXIV (1923), pp. 60-2 and O. G. S. Crawford: *Air Survey and Archaeology* (1924), p. 6.

For an excellent discussion of classical writings and their worth (also with references) see:

A. L. F. Rivet: *Town and Country in Roman Britain* (1958), pp. 16-22.

See also:

S. S. Frere's review of this book in *Antiquity*, XXXIII (1959), p. 67, for a variant reading of Diodorus Siculus' passage about corn storage.

*Illuminating commentaries on farming practice at the beginning of our era* (not all necessarily of application in Britain) are to be found in:

Columella: *Res rustica* Loeb Edition (1940-4).

Pliny the Elder—*Natural History*, Loeb Edition (1940). (Especially book XVIII, on cereal agriculture.)

Varro: *Rerum rusticarum libri tres.* Translated: Lloyd Storr-Best (Bohn's Classical Library) 1912. (This was a practical handbook, written at the age of 80 for his wife.)

Siculus Flaccus: as quoted by V Seebohm 1890, p. 277. (1926 reprint.)

II. *SOME EARLY REFERENCES TO ANCIENT FIELDS IN THIS COUNTRY AND ORIGIN OF LYNCHETS*

1776    Wm. Stukeley, *Itinerarium Curiosum* (2nd Ed.), Iter VII, pp. 188–9 (describes "balks or meres of ploughed lands . . . too small . . . unless of the most Ancient Britons" near Blandford).

1812    R. Colt Hoare, *Ancient Wiltshire* I, p. 69 n. (describes *strip lynchets* caused by the effect of the plough on sloping ground).

1836    Wm. Cobbett, *Rural Rides* (Everyman's Library), Vol. II, pp. 81–2.

1869    Poulett Scrope: *W.A.M.*, XII, p. 186 (describes his observation of modern lynchet formation to confute the theory that they were raised sea beaches).

        Wm. Cunnington, *ibid.* p. 191 (describes robbing of lynchets for flints).

III. *THE GROWTH OF MODERN RECOGNITION OF TYPES*
   *General Studies on Ancient Agriculture*

1902    R. Blaker: *Sx. A.C.*, XLV, pp. 198–203 (first argued the existence of fields dissimilar from strip lynchets and suggested that they were "the corn fields to which the Roman Chronicles" referred).

1911    H. S. Toms, *The Antiquary* (November 1911, pp. 411–17. "The problem of ancient cultivations.")

1923    O. G. S. Crawford, *Geog. J.*, LXI, pp. 342–66 (reprinted in *Air Survey and Archaeology*, O.S. Professional Paper No. 7). E. and E. Cecil Curwen, *Sx. A.C.*, LXIV, pp. 1–65. *Note.*—The two papers above proclaimed the authors' independent but similar conclusions on the class of fields called for the first time "Celtic".

1924    O. G. S. Crawford, *Air Survey and Archaeology*. O.S. Professional Paper No. 7.

1927    E. Cecil Curwen, *A.*, I, pp. 261–89. (Prehistoric Agriculture.)

1932    E. Cecil Curwen, (*a*) *A.*, VI, pp. 389–406 ("Ancient Cultivations"); (*b*) Congress of Archaeological Societies, 39th Report, pp. 30–5 and 41–3 (report on lynchets and grass ridges).

1935    G. A. Holleyman, *A.*, IX, pp. 443–54. ("The 'Celtic' field system in South Britain" based on work in Sussex.)

1936    C. A. Ralegh Radford, *Ox.*, I. (Ditchley villa and a consideration of its attributed acreage based on granary capacity.)

1938     E. C. Curwen, (a) Air photography and the evolution of the cornfield; (b) The early development of agriculture in Britain. *P.P.S.*, IV, pp. 27–52.

Evert Barger, *E.H.R.*, CCXI, pp. 385 ff. ("The present position of studies in English field systems.")

1946     E. Cecil Curwen, *Plough and Pasture*.

1947     C.B.A., *Survey and Policy*.

1952     M. D. Nightingale, *Arch. Cant.*, LXV, pp. 150–9 (embodying an excellent description of *centuriation* by C. E. Stevens).

1952     J. G. D. Clark, *Prehistoric Europe: the economic background*, Chaps. IV and V.

1955     H. C. Bowen, *A.N.L.*, 6, pp. 36 ff. ("The problem of Roman Villa Fields", reprinted in C.B.A. research report No. 1).

1958     S. Applebaum, *A.H.R.*, VI, pp. 66–86. ("Agriculture in Roman Britain.")

(Ed.) H. C. Bowen, *A. of S.*, 56 (March), pp. 365–71. (Summary of papers read to the Dublin Conference, 1957, by A. Aberg, "Introduction to Ancient Ploughs"; H. C. Bowen, "The study of ancient fields"; P. Flatrès, "Rural patterns in Celtic countries"; V. B. Proudfoot, "Ancient Irish Field systems".)

## IV. IMPLEMENTS AND TECHNIQUES
### i. Ploughs

1914     A. S. F. Gow, *Journal of Hellenic Studies*, XXXIV, pp. 249–75.

1932     G. W. B. Huntingford, *A.*, VI, pp. 327–37 (considers Roman writings on ploughing in the light of experience in modern Kenya).

1938     C. W. Phillips, *P.P.S.*, IV, p. 338. (Guardstones for plough mould-boards.)

1947     F. G. Payne, *Arch. J.*, CIV, pp. 82–111. ("The Plough in early Britain.")

1951     P. V. Glob, *Plov og Ard i nordens oldtid* (with English summary, pp. 109–33) is an excellent and very well illustrated detail account of prehistoric ploughs in north Europe.

1952     G. E. Fussell, *The Farmer's Tools* (A.D. 1500–1900) (not restricted to ploughs).

1953     M. Nightingale, *A.*, XXVII, pp. 20 ff. ("Ploughing and field shape.")

1954     C. Singer (Ed.), *History of Technology*, I, pp. 539 ff. (Earliest Agriculture) (by M. S. Drower).

II, pp. 81 ff. (Subsequent development of agricultural implements) (by E. M. Jope).

1956    R. Aitken, *J.R.S.*, XLVI, pp. 97 ff. ("Virgil's plough.")

1956–7  F. A. Aberg, *Gwerin*, I, pp. 171–81. ("The early plough in Europe.")

1957    F. G. Payne, *A.H.R.*, V, pp. 74–84. (The British plough: some stages in its development.)

1957–8  A. Steensberg, *Folk-Liv.*, pp. 157–62. ("Parallel ploughing with alternately sloping and upright ard in Columella.")

1960    A. Steensberg, Selected Papers of the 5th International Congress of anthropological and ethnological sciences (Sep. 1956), pp. 342–5. (Plough and field shape.)

## ii. *Cereals*

1944    K. Jessen and H. Helbaek, "Cereals in Great Britain and Ireland in Prehistoric and Early Historic Times". (*Kgl. Dan. Vidensk Selsk. Biol. Skrifter.*)

1952    H. Helbaek, *P.P.S.*, XVIII, pp. 194–233. ("Early Crops in South Britain.")
        (*N.B.*—The two works above are complementary.)

1954    J. R. B. Arthur, *Sx. A.C.*, 91, pp. 37–47. (Prehistoric wheats in Sussex.)

## iii. *Harvesting implements*

1943    Axel Steensberg, *Ancient harvesting implements.* A study in archaeology and human geography. (Complementary to VI Hatt 1951.)

## iv. *Threshing*

1935    O. G. S. Crawford, *A.*, IX, pp. 335–9 (note on the "tribulum", a wooden sledge set with flints of a probably characteristic form).

## v. *Corn drying*

1943    R. G. Goodchild, *Ant. J.*, XXIII, pp. 148 ff. (Romano-British T-shaped ovens).

1951    Lindsay Scott, *A.*, XXV, pp. 196–208 ("Corn-drying kilns", embracing a study of those in recent use).

1958    E. M. Jope and R. I. Threlfall, *Mediaeval Archaeology*, II, pp. 123–4 (in the description of an excavated thirteenth-century corn-growing settlement in modern moorland of Beere, N. Tawton, Devon).

## vi. *Querns*

1937    E. C. Curwen, *A.*, XI, pp. 133–51.

1941    E. C. Curwen, *A.*, XV, pp. 15–32.

1950    J. Phillips, *T.L.A.S.*, pp. 75 ff.

1951    L. H. Butcher, *Trans. Hunter Arch. Soc.*, VII, pp. 38–9 (preliminary note of a quern factory).

V. *STRIP LYNCHETS, OPEN-FIELDS, ETC.* (*See also Sections III and V*)

1890　　　F. Seebohm, *The English Village Community*. (4th Ed.)

1915　　　H. L. Gray, *English Field Systems*

1939　　　E. Cecil Curwen, *A.*, XIII, pp. 45–52. ("The plough and the origin of 'Strip Lynchets'.")

1949　　　H. P. R. Finberg, *A.*, XXIII, pp. 180–7. ("The open fields in Devonshire.")

　　　　　H. J. E. Peake and J. M. Birkbeck, *N.D.F.C.T.*, VII, pp. 6–11. ("Terrace cultivation at East Garston, Berks.")

1952　　　A. E. P. Collins, *B.A.J.*, LIII, pp. 57–8. (Excavation of strip lynchets lying over the remains of a hillfort on Blewburton Hill.)

1954　　　C. S. and C. S. Orwin, *The Open Fields* (2nd Ed.) (Includes a detailed study of the surviving open-field system at Laxton, Notts. The Appendix, on the "origin of lynchets", which in substance appeared in the first edition (1938), doubts the arable origin or use of strip lynchets. The argument was considered in detail by Curwen (1939) above.)

　　　　　H. C. Darby, *A.H.R.*, II, pp. 30 ff. ("Some early ideas on the agricultural regions of England.")

　　　　　A. Austin Miller, *A. of S.*, 43, pp. 277 ff. (a consideration of strip lynchets in the very early stages of notable research by the Department of Geography, Reading University).

1955　　　P. D. Wood, *W.A.M.*, 56, pp. 12–16. (The Excavation of strip lynchets at Bishopstone, near Swindon, Wiltshire.)

　　　　　R. H. Hilton, *A.H.R.*, III, pp. 3–19. ("The content and sources of English agrarian history before 1500.")

　　　　　J. Thirsk, *A.H.R.*, III, pp. 66–79. ("The content and sources of English agrarian history after 1500.")

1958　　　P. D. Wood, *W.A.M.*, 57, pp. 18–24 (second excavation at Bishopstone).

1959　　　P. D. Wood and G. Whittington, *W.A.M.*, 57, pp. 163–72. (The excavation and consideration of strip lynchets north of the Vale of Pewsey.)

1960　　　P. D. Wood and G. Whittington, *W.A.M.*, 57, pp. 322–38 (further examination of the above).

VI. *RIDGE-AND-FURROW, OPEN FIELDS, ETC.*

1890　　　E. Lamond (Ed.), *Walter of Henley's "Husbandry"*.

1935　　　*A.*, IX, pp. 89–90 (shows *broad rig* over "Celtic" fields on chalk downland, Thornham Down, Wiltshire).

1948　　　M. W. Beresford, *Econ. H.R.* (2nd series), I, pp. 34 ff. ("Ridge-and-furrow and the open fields.")

1951   E. Kerridge, *Econ. H.R.* (2nd series), IV, pp. 14–36. ("Ridge-and-furrow and agrarian history.")

1954   W. R. Mead, *Geog. J.*, CXX, Ridge-and-furrow in Bucks.

1955   E. Kerridge, *A.H.R.*, III, pp. 26–40 (discusses ridge-and-furrow and boundary balks).

      S. R. Eyre, *A.H.R.*, III, pp. 80 ff. ("The curving plough strip and its historical implications.")

1956   H. A. Beecham, *A.H.R.*, IV, pp. 22 ff. ("A review of balks as strip boundaries in the open fields.")

*Note.*—The widespread existence of ridge-and-furrow in chalk country, not generally recognised, is further indicated by reference to III Crawford 1924, Plate V; VIII Crawford and Keiller 1928, Plates XIX, XX, XXIb, XXII and XLIX. See also III Bowen 1955.

## STUDIES OF REGIONS AND SITES (*VII–XIX*)

*Note.*—No attempt has been made to be exhaustive. Many works not listed here are referred to in the area studies and in those listed in III and IV above. The county or local archaeological society's annual volumes are likely to have notes of all sites investigated in their areas. Index volumes are often available to help in the search. Since 1946 the C.B.A. have produced admirable annual archaeological bibliographies for Great Britain and Ireland indexed topographically and by subject. Before the war the Congress of Archaeological Studies also provided very useful periodical notes.

### Overall distribution of "Celtic" fields

1956   O.S. Map of Roman Britain, 3rd Ed. (shows areas of all known "Celtic" fields throughout Britain whether specifically Roman or not).

1958   I. A. Richmond (Ed.), *Roman and Native in North Britain*. Chapter I, by S. Piggott, "Native economies and the Roman occupation of North Britain."

### Southern Britain

**VII.** *SUSSEX.* Particularly rich in remains and to date better recorded than in any other county. For references see:

1954   E. C. Curwen, *Prehistory of Sussex*.

1957   G. P. Burstow and G. A. Holleyman, *P.P.S.*, XXIII, pp. 167–212. ("Late Bronze Age settlement on Itford Hill, Sussex"; important though no contemporary fields had survived.)

VIII. *WESSEX*

1924   O. G. S. Crawford, *Air Survey and Archaeology*; end folders
       show "Celtic" fields on Figheldean Down (Wilts. 6-inch
       O.S. map XLVIII, S.W.) and in central Hants (map scale
       1:20,000), both plotted from air photographs.

1928   O. G. S. Crawford and A. Keiller, *Wessex from the Air*.

       O. G. S. Crawford, *A.*, II, pp. 173–87 ("Our debt to Rome?":
       a study of Romano-British and Saxon settlement distribu-
       tion in N.E. Dorset and parts of S. Wilts.).

1931   C. W. Phillips, *U.B.S.S.*, IV, p. 34. (Walton Down.)

1933   C. W. Phillips, *U.B.S.S.*, IV, p. 139. (Failand Ridge and
       Wraxall areas N.E. of Bristol.)

1933   O.S. Map: "Celtic earthworks of Salisbury Plain"(1:25,000)
       Sheet I (Old Sarum); (Amesbury, Sheet 2, was completed
       but not published; 4 other sheets were planned).

1936   J. D. M. Stuart and J. M. Birkbeck, *H.F.C.P.*, XIII, pp. 188–
       207. ("Celtic village on Twyford Down", including an
       attempt to date a strip field to the Belgic period.)

1939   C. F. C. Hawkes, *H.F.C.P.*, XIV, pp. 136–194. (Excavations
       at Quarley Hill, basic to any study of linear ditches con-
       temporary with "Celtic" fields.)

1940   G. Bersu, *P.P.S.*, VI, pp. 30–111. ("Excavations at Little
       Woodbury, Wilts." essential to the understanding of
       certain Iron Age agricultural practices, though no fields
       had survived.)

1947   C. F. C. Hawkes and S. Piggott, *A.J.* CIV, pp. 27–81.("Britons,
       Romans and Saxons in Cranborne Chase", an important
       re-examination of Pitt-Rivers' excavations with reflections
       on agrarian development.)

1948   C. M. Piggott, *P.P.S.*, VIII, p. 48. ("Five Late Bronze Age
       enclosures in North Wiltshire": includes a consideration of
       agricultural remains of the period.)

1951   P. P. Rhodes, *Ox.*, XV, pp. 1–28. (The "Celtic" field
       systems on the Berkshire Downs.)

       R.C.H.M. Dorset I (later volumes will treat ancient fields
       more fully).

1954   S. Applebaum, *P.P.S.*, XX, pp. 103–14, cf. III Crawford,
       1924. ("The agriculture of the British early Iron Age as
       exemplified at Figheldean Down, Wiltshire", a stimulating
       interpretation of "Celtic" field and enclosure remains
       which stresses the need for analytical ground surveys.)

1955    H. P. R. Finberg, *Roman and Saxon Withington (Glos.): a study in continuity* (University College of Leicester, Department of Eng. Local Hist., Occ. Paper No. 8).

1957    *V.C.H., Wiltshire*, I, part (1), pp. 272–9; a gazetteer of sites.

1960    W. F. Grimes, *Excavations on Defence sites* 1939–45, I. ("Celtic" fields on Charmy Down, nr. Bath.)

Forth-   R.C.H.M. Dorset II–IV.
coming

## IX. SOUTH-WEST ENGLAND

1938    A. H. Shorter, *A*, XII, pp. 183–9. ("Ancient fields in Manaton parish, Dartmoor.")

1941    D. Dudley, *A.J.*, XCVIII, pp. 105–30. (Trewey Downs, Zennor.)

1951    *P.D.A.E.S.*, IV, pp. 102–5 (a further note).

1952    C. A. Ralegh Radford, *P.P.S.*, XVIII, pp. 55–84. ("Prehistoric Settlements on Dartmoor and the Cornish moors.")

1954    Aileen Fox, *P.P.S.*, XX, pp. 87–102. ("Celtic" fields and farms on Dartmoor.)

1957    D. Dudley, *Journal of the Royal Institute of Cornwall*, 3, I, pp. 66–82. (Zennor.)

## X. SOUTH-EAST ENGLAND

1948    E. Greenfield, C. W. Meates and W. Birchenough, *Arch. Cant.*, LXI, pp. 180–3. (Lynchets in Farningham–Shoreham area of Kent.)

1952    B. Hope-Taylor, *Sy. A.C.*, 50, pp. 47–72. (" 'Celtic' agriculture in Surrey.")

## XI. WELSH MARCHES

1954    O. G. S. Crawford, *A.*, XXVIII, pp. 168–9. (Long Mynd, Shropshire.)

## XII. NORTH ENGLAND

1929    A. Raistrick and S. E. Chapman, *A.*, III, pp. 165–81. ("The lynchet groups of Upper Wharfedale.")

1930    F. Elgee, *Early man in N.E. Yorkshire*.

1931    W. P. Hedley, *A.*, V, pp. 351–4. (Cultivation remains at Housesteads.)

          *Liverpool Annals*, *XXIV*, pp. 156 ff. (takes a different view of the above, very interesting, complex).

1937   A. Raistrick, (*Prehistoric cultivations at Grassington, W. Yorks.*).
       *Y.A.J.*, XXXIII, pp. 166–74; cf. also *J.R.S.*, XL (1950),
       Pl. VI (1).
1938   R.C.H.M., Westmorland.
1954   J. D. Bu'Lock, L. and C.A.S. (Possible "Celtic" fields in
       Lancashire.)
1956   M. Posnansky, *D.A.J.*, 76, p. 71. (Note on the presence of
       prehistoric field systems in Derbyshire.)
1957   J. Wilfred Jackson, *D.A.J.* LXXVII, pp. 62–3. (Note on current
       investigation at Priestcliffe, nr. Taddington, Derby.)

## XIII. EAST ANGLIA

1938   E. C. Curwen, *P.P.S.*, IV, p. 46. (Crop marks of apparent
       strip fields related to Romano-British structures.)
1946   D. N. Riley, *A.*, XIX, pp. 145–53. (An aerial reconnaissance.)
1949   J. G. D. Clark, *Ant. J.*, 29, pp. 145–63. (Romano-British site
       at Cottenham, Cambs.: associated with "Celtic" fields.)
1951   W. F. Grimes (Ed.). *Aspects of archaeology in Britain and beyond*,
       pp. 258–73. ("The Fenland research Committee", by C. W.
       Phillips.)

## XIV. RIVER GRAVELS OF ENGLAND

1943–4 D. N. Riley, *Archaeology from the air in the Upper Thames
       valley.*
1960   R.C.H.M., *A matter of Time.* (A Field Archaeology of the
       River Gravels of England.)

## XV. WALES

1937   B. H. St. J. O'Neill, *Ant. J.*, XVI. (Caerau, Clynnog,
       Caernarvonshire, remains akin to "Celtic" fields around
       Romano-British houses.)
1940   R.C.A.M. (Wales) Anglesey (reprinted with additions 1960).
1952   W. F. Grimes, *Arch. Camb.*, CI. (The field archaeology of
       Skomer Island, Pembs.)
1958   R.C.A.M. (Wales), Caernarvon I.

## XVI. SCOTLAND

1938   A. Graham, *P.S.A.S.*, 73. (Cultivation terraces in S.E.
       Scotland.)
1956   R.C.A.M. (Scotland), Roxburgh.

XVII. *IRELAND*
    1958    V. B. Proudfoot, *A. of S.*, 56, pp. 369–71 (with bibliography).

XVIII. *DENMARK*
    1951    G. Hatt, *Oldtidsagre* (with English summary). (An important and detailed survey of "Celtic" fields in Jutland. "Oldtidsagre" is the name first used by Sophus Müller for "Celtic" fields in Denmark.)

XIX. *HOLLAND*
    1928    A. E. van Giffen, *A.*, II, pp. 85–7. ("Celtic" fields on Noordse Veld, near Zeijen.)

XX. *AERIAL PHOTOGRAPHY AND SURVEY*
    *See* III Crawford 1924.
    1929    O. G. S. Crawford, *Air photography for archaeologists*. (O.S. Professional Paper No. 12 with some excellent air photographs of Wessex sites.)
    1938    O. G. S. Crawford, *Luftbild und Vorgeschichte*. (A Luft-Hansa publication—with British and Continent sites.)
    1944    D. N. Riley, *Arch. J.*, CI, pp. 1–16. ("The technique of air-archaeology", based on wartime flying experience.)
    1947    K. A. Steer, *A.*, XXI, pp. 50–3. ("Archaeology and the National air-photograph survey.")
    1948    D. B. Harden, *A guide to an exhibition of Air Photographs of Archaeological Sites*. (Ashmolean Museum.)
    1950    Lyle G. Trorey, *A handbook of aerial mapping and photogrammetry*.
    1951    W. F. Grimes (Ed.), *Aspects of archaeology in Britain*, pp. 303–15. ("A survey of pioneering in air photography past and future" by J. K. St. Joseph.)
            J. K. S. St. Joseph, *J.R.S.*, XLI, pp. 52–65. ("Air reconnaissance of Northern Britain.")
    1953    R. J. C. Atkinson, *Field Archaeology* (2nd Ed.) ("Archaeological Survey", pp. 85 ff.)
    1957    J. S. P. Bradford, *Ancient Landscapes* (includes detailed accounts of how to use—and take—aerial photographs. Chap. IV is an excellent introduction to centuriation).
    (in progress) J. K. S. St. Joseph, *Catalogue of Cambridge University Collection of Aerial Photographs*, Part I (1951) XVI (1959), *in progress*. (This covers all photographs taken in the period 1945–55 arranged in their order of taking.)

PLATES I to V

PLATE I

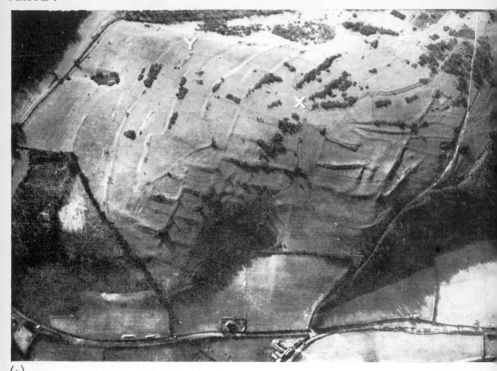

(a)

(b)

PLATE I

"Celtic" fields, *Shillingstone Hill, Dorset (cf. frontispiece).*

(a)  Near-vertical air photograph by the R.A.F. *Crown Copyright reserved.* North to the bottom. Before ploughing. Some secondary strip plough-marks particularly clear left and right of centre. *Double-lynchet way* in top right quarter. Some lynchets below this appear as close-set double lines because the flints have been dug out all along them. "X" and "Y" as in frontispiece. Approximate distance XY is 400 yds.

(b)  View of north side of Shillingstone Hill looking south-west from the north-western corner of the Roman fort inside the Iron Age hillfort of Hod Hill. Photograph by R.C.H.M.(Eng.). *Crown Copyright reserved.*

PLATE II

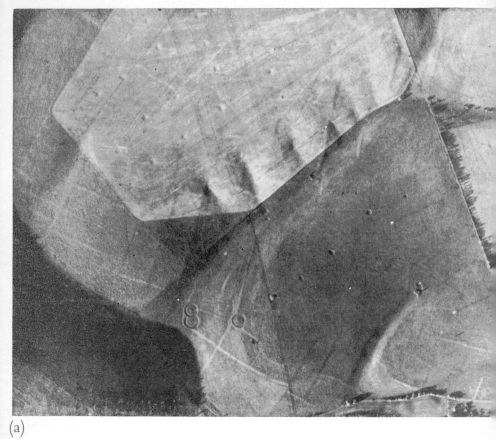

(a)

PLATE II

(a)  Grafton, Wilts., near Scots Poor. One inch O.S. Sheet 167 Nat. Grid. Ref.
271563. Near vertical photograph by the R.A.F. *Crown Copyright reserved.*
North to the top.

Disc barrows left bottom of centre seem to be on "Celtic" lynchets but
are not. (See p. 30 and fig. 2E.) A single bowl barrow is seen right of the three
discs: a line of marl pits runs top right from this significantly in an area devoid
of "Celtic" fields whose remains have probably been destroyed in relatively
recent times. The light-coloured area in the top of the photograph is modern
stubble. Lines of marl pits are again visible. Distance from centre of bowl
barrow to centre of larger of intersecting discs is c. 250 yds.

(b)  *Narrow-rig* north of Portesham Withy Bed, Dorset, in a compact block in an
area of "Celtic" fields and *strip-lynchets*. It can be shown to be later than
both. (Cf. p. 47.) Photograph by R.C.H.M.(Eng.). *Crown copyright reserved.*

PLATE III

PLATE III

*South of Kingston, Corfe Castle, Dorset.* One inch O.S. sheet 178 Nat. Grid. Ref. 957780. Near vertical air photograph by R.A.F. *Crown copyright reserved.* North to the top.

Two settlements with remains of contemporary, but disturbed, "Celtic" fields around them. On a limestone spur. The first settlement is in the centre, shaped like a flask on its side with the mouth to the left. The second, south-east of this, is in the angle contained by the deep shadow of the re-entrant and the "shine" mark of the south-east face of the spur. Much of the area to the top of the picture, where the "Celtic" fields have been largely destroyed, bears traces of *broad rig*, again obvious left of the first settlement. It is suggested that the straight lynchet running north-south divides two farms (see p. 36). The field divisions were probably limestone walls. "X" lies against a contemporary track running east to the second settlement. Distance from "X" north along the probable ancient boundary to the modern stone wall is approx. 570 yds.

PLATE IV

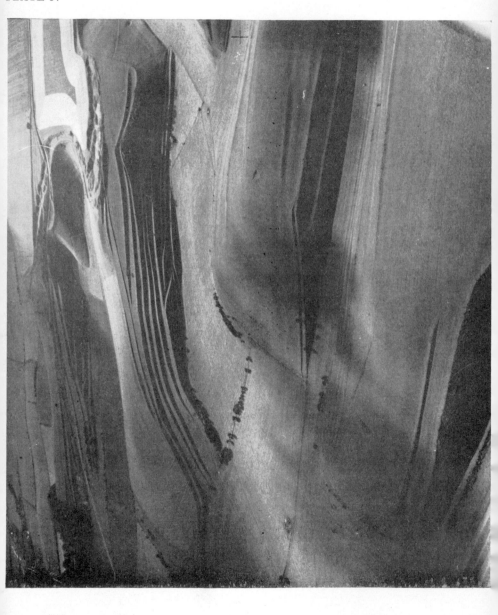

# PLATE IV. KEY

(a) Strip lynchets with small trees growing on the faces of the risers.

(b) A secondary negative lynchet cuts across the ends of (a). Note the gap between this and the prominent riser above. Immediately to the right of (b) is a sharp modern negative lynchet and it seems that one *strip lynchet* was levelled before ploughing.

(c) Modern plough furrows. These end on the south against a modern headland with a positive lynchet about one foot high.

(d) Traces of "Celtic" fields. The relatively short riser running left to right ends at a point where rounded scarps run at right angles to it. Where exposed in the pit at (d) the scarp consists of solid chalk, the "positive" element ploughed away.

(e) Is a block of *narrow rig*, each ridge 4½ yards wide and 6 inches high.

(f) Access ramps, most of which seem to have been ploughed.

(g) The *strip lynchets* here narrow first to 7 ft. and then to 4 ft. and one continues at this width for 50 yards before ending in a point. It is difficult to imagine how a plough could have turned.

(h) No strip lynchets on this steep north facing slope, but two up and down scarps clearer on the air photograph than on the ground. Possibly divisions of the "Celtic" phase.

(j) A low bank and ditch cut by the negative lynchets on the valley floor.

(k) A field being harvested. Note the diagonal marks.

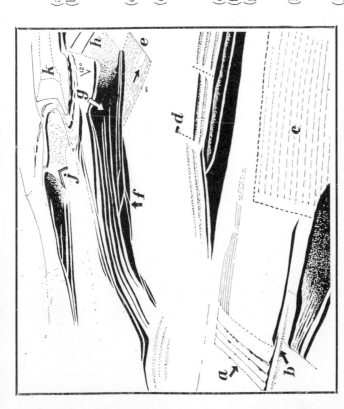

*Strip Lynchets, Mere, Wilts. (Crown copyright reserved) N.G.R. 825335*

This superb air photograph by Dr. St. Joseph was taken from the east. Representative points are noted on the explanatory diagram; others of a similar kind can be found by close examination. Although the *strip lynchets* are dominant there are traces of a number of other types of arable remains representing phases from "Celtic" to the present.

PLATE V

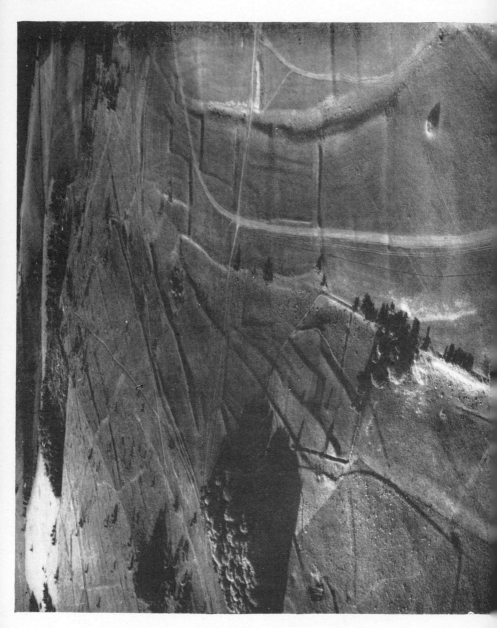

PLATE V

*Fyfield Down, Near Marlborough, Wilts.* One inch O.S. sheet 157 Nat. Grid. Ref. c. 140708. This is a new low-level oblique air photograph by Dr. J. K. St. Joseph, taken from the south, of an area sometimes illustrated as "typical 'Celtic' fields". Most of it was indeed covered by "Celtic" fields but an unconformable system of *open-field* strips, marked by *broad rig* and occasional slightly-developed *strip-lynchets* blankets a large part of the area. An archaeological study is being made by P. J. Fowler and H. C. Bowen and will be published in W.A.M.

(Cf. p. 49.)

# INDEX

1/71